WITHOUT A TRACE

The Life of Sierra Phantom

Danielle Nadler

NEW YORK

LONDON • NASHVILLE • MELBOURNE • VANCOUVER

Without A Trace

The Life of Sierra Phantom

Published in New York, New York, by Morgan James Publishing. Morgan James is a trademark of Morgan James, LLC. www.MorganJamesPublishing.com

The Morgan James Speakers Group can bring authors to your live event. For more information or to book an event visit The Morgan James Speakers Group at www.TheMorganJamesSpeakersGroup.com.

ISBN 9781683507895 paperback
ISBN 9781683507901 eBook
Library of Congress Control Number: 2017915424

Cover Design by:
Nathaniel Navratil

Interior Design by:
Paul Curtis

Photographs of Sierra Phantom by:
Trevor Woods

Author photograph by:
Douglas Graham

In an effort to support local communities, raise awareness and funds, Morgan James Publishing donates a percentage of all book sales for the life of each book to Habitat for Humanity Peninsula and Greater Williamsburg.

Get involved today! Visit
www.MorganJamesBuilds.com

For my father, the late Robert MacMurchy,
who taught me the power of a story well lived.

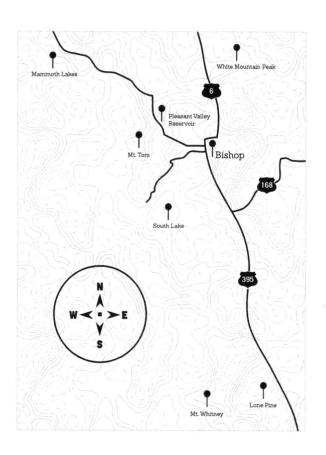

Table of Contents

"I've always had a real passion for nature. The thing that kept me going is the mystique of it. I grew up with a curious mind, wondering what's behind that next mountain, what's up there, what's down there. I've always been that way. I'm still that way today."

— Sierra Phantom, December 2011

PREFACE

I'm really not an author. I'm a journalist.

That's the line I clung to when I was first asked to write a book. I'd made a quiet pact with myself years earlier that I would never attempt such a conquest.

It was a college professor's PowerPoint presentation that led to this unspoken agreement. The scrawny, sweatered sixty-something paraded disheartening statistics about the likelihood of any of the undeclared freshmen under his watch having their work published. I think his lectures were carefully crafted to weed out those who loved the idea of becoming the next J.K. Rowling more than the written word itself.

But for me, it was just the nudge I needed to refocus my ambitions where they'd been since I was fifteen years old. I wanted to be a journalist. Specifically, a newspaper reporter. And that publishing class got me thinking: well, why not when you get to write with a practical guarantee that your work will be read in black and white the following day?

Now, fifteen years later, my work that's filed by 9 o'clock each evening is tossed in thousands of driveways throughout three Virginia counties before I can get in a full night's sleep. It's all virtually old news by the time I'm back at my desk to file another day's worth of articles.

The publishing side of journalism is beautifully uncomplicated. And I've never had a reason to pursue anything different, no reason to break that pact. Until I heard a story I couldn't walk away from. A story that would hold my attention far beyond the 24-hour news cycle. A story that changed me.

My friend Craig called me one night during my commute home from the newsroom. He teaches high school agriculture in California and is the most spontaneous person I know—as in, he's asked me out of the blue more than once, "You want to go to Australia next week?" Or Spain or Italy or wherever he'd been dreaming of that day. He yelled through the phone in his coarse accent, "MacMurchy . . ."—he still calls me by my maiden name to remind me we share Scottish roots—"I've got a book idea for you. Ya have to write about this guy!" At first, I considered it another of his impossible proposals.

I bluntly reminded him that I'm not that kind of writer. But he talked over any objections I raised and launched into this story about an old mountaineer he'd met a few days earlier while on a hike. "That's just the start of it," he announced through the phone after giving me the ten-cent version of this stranger's life story. "Will you do it?"

"Well, I'll call him I guess," I said, offering just enough to get Craig off the phone. "No guarantees, though."

The next evening, exhausted after another day of scrambling to make deadline, I paced my bedroom and reluctantly called this man who went by the fantastical name Sierra Phantom.

Less than an hour later, I sat on the edge of my bed in silence. My eyes opened wide, and my mouth hung open. I had to share this.

"Are you willing to keep talking to me, maybe once a week or so?" I asked the old man as we wrapped up our first conversation.

"Oh yeah. People have always told me I should write a book about all I've seen and done, but I've never been any good at knowin' where the commas and the periods and all that go."

"Mr. Phantom, all you have to do is share your story," I told him, suddenly agreeing to begin this impossible task. "I would love to add the commas and the periods."

CHAPTER

Non-native

(adj.) A species living outside its native habitat.

May Day 1935, Lake Washington

MOST KIDS CAN TELL YOU not long into elementary school how they got their name. Maybe their old man named them after a grandparent, or their mother called them after her favorite city or character from the history books. But his childhood was different. For him, those parts of life, the stuff usually shared around the kitchen table, were mostly not known. The little that was documented was kept in a manila folder that followed him wherever the State of California, and later the State of Washington, moved him.

He started out as John P. Glover. He was never told what the P stood for. By his second orphanage it became J.P. Glover and then just Glover by his third. When he was old enough to come up with something better, he did. He settled on the kind of name that doesn't get dropped into an introduction without being followed by a request for the story behind it. It was May Day 1935 when his birth name first appeared in print beyond that incomplete government file. An article in a community newspaper just outside of Seattle made mention of the boy. It wasn't for anything that would qualify as a Page 1 story. Not a car crash or house fire. Nothing to do with the Great Depression, which had left a quarter of the state's population unemployed that year. It was a couple of insignificant paragraphs tucked back near the classifieds, no doubt meant to fill a news hole during a slow week. But in Glover's mind, those few lines, permanently stamped in black ink onto dingy newsprint, documented something much greater.

It all happened at the Luther Burbank School for Boys' May Day Field Day, an annual gathering that had become a platform for the orphans to flex their physical capabilities and have a bit of fun. The boys could enter as many events as they wanted. Each first-place win earned them two points, and they got one point for second place. Whoever tallied the most points got a trip into town with the headmaster for a movie or an ice cream or a trip to the comic book store—whichever they might want to do for an afternoon.

At first, Glover signed up for one swimming event just to give it a go. He settled on the fifty-yard freestyle, for no reason other than it was set to begin within the next few minutes. Just before the starting gun blasted, as the five other boys crouched in athletic stances ready to launch themselves into the water, the eight-year-old tapped the shoulder of the older boy next to him and admitted that he had no idea what he was expected to do in the event. The older boy shook his head and quickly explained through clenched teeth that the type of stroke didn't matter, as long as he swam the total distance. And then Glover heard the blast.

His feet hit the chilly lake water first, followed by his thin frame and uncombed, dirty blond hair. The sting of cold seemed to jump start him into action. With eyes closed and breath held, his arms and legs began to churn. His feet, from the tips of his toes to his ankle, kicked while his arms flew above the water, then below, again and again like a propeller that had come to life. Every few strokes he allowed himself time to pull in a breath of spring air, which he pushed out below the water, sending bubbles into the depths of Lake Washington to disappear at the surface an instant after the boy had passed.

About three-fourths of the way through the event, as Glover took in another gulp of oxygen, he noticed not one swimmer was near him. He thought he'd been left in everyone's wake, but he didn't care. He had discovered it, some new feeling. Invigoration. He soaked it in as if it were fuel and pushed each inch of his body to keep working until he reached the finish line at the dock. His right hand reached out for the dock just as he looked back to discover the other boys in the race still had another twenty yards to go. He had pulled ahead of every one of them, including those who were three and four years older. He'd beaten them by a long shot.

He entered and won every other swimming event the meet offered that day: twenty-five-yard backstroke, 100-yard freestyle. He even outpaced the competition in a diving contest off a springboard that was bolted to the dock. After each win, someone appeared to hand him another plastic blue ribbon, which he tossed near his towel before hurrying back to the water for the next event. It wasn't about the win, or even the act of swimming. It certainly wasn't about a trip to the comic book store. It was something else. In those few moments when he couldn't hear or see what was waiting for him on the shore—overweight bullies, hairy-chinned headmistresses, chores and thin pea soup—all of his other senses felt more alive.

As he came out of the water after the final event, a man from the local newspaper approached him and wrapped a towel around his shoulders. "You left the other kids in your dust," he yelled down to young Glover as if he thought the water had obstructed the boy's hearing. "How did you do it, son?"

He looked up toward the reporter, his lungs still catching up with the rest of him. "I don't know," he said, honestly.

"How long have you been training for this?" the man yelled, digging for a good quote for his article no doubt.

"I haven't, sir. I wasn't competing against anybody, really," the boy said. "I was competing against myself."

"Oh yeah," the reporter looked down at the boy while his black pen, unsupervised, scribbled over the narrow notebook clenched in his right hand. "Well, waddya mean by that, kid?"

"What I'm sayin' is it's not about being first. I've just always wanted to go faster, to go higher," the boy squinted through the late afternoon sun to look straight into the man's eyes. "To feel free."

At that, the man's pen stopped mid-sentence. He looked down at the orphan as if he was out of words. His lips formed a narrow smile, one that seemed more sad than happy. He bowed his head slightly as he put his hat back in place and walked away.

Glover knew what it was that had stolen any words the man may have been ready to deliver. He had witnessed the kid behind the stormy blue eyes come to life. It was as if there was something magical in that lake water. As though the region's highest peaks, from which the spring runoff had trickled down and come to immerse him that afternoon, were now drawing him in.

From that moment on, Glover maintained an ever-evolving escape plan. He kept his eye out for unlocked gates, unattended trucks, or, at one orphanage years later, an unsupervised rowboat, to help set his strategy into motion. He'd hide biscuits in his bunk for whenever he might get the gall to run. Plenty of nights he gave it a go, but he was usually spotted by a nosy neighbor or a police officer who promptly returned the scrawny kid to his assigned guardians. Between attempts to flee, he'd hide out in the attic's rafters until boredom or hunger drew him out, just to prove more to himself than anyone else that he couldn't be contained. On afternoons when most in the orphanage were distracted with work, he could be spotted lying on his back in the dirt just beyond the property line staring up at the sky, as if it looked bluer from the other side of the fence.

"Being free was all I wanted," he would later say. "It became like a magnet."

More than seventy years later, an older version of that boy sat on a thrift store couch in a California mountain town, with a cigarette perched in one hand and a phone in the other. I sat quietly on the other end of the line and listened. He told me that story, followed by a hundred others, each bringing into view a life lived like none I'd ever heard. His stories, all taken together, are the best explanation for how he got that name: Sierra Phantom.

CHAPTER

Snag

(n.) An unexpected obstacle or hindrance.

(v.) To catch a fish.

Present day, Bishop, California

ALMOST EXACTLY A YEAR BEFORE Glover outswam every boy in the tri-county area at that May Day meet, a government employee failed to put out a cigarette in one of California's state buildings. It happened to be a building where they kept the children's services records. Firefighters from four area departments responded but couldn't stop most of the place from burning to the ground and taking Glover's manila folder with it.

It wasn't until he was seventy-three years old, shortly before our paths crossed, that he found himself wishing for the first time that he'd had that folder. He sat in a whitewashed Social Security office on Line Street in Bishop, California, thinking up a way to string together enough official documentation to prove his existence to a government he swore he'd rid himself of.

HIS THIN FRAME took a beating sitting in that metal chair all afternoon. Sierra Phantom hunched over a clipboard stacked an inch thick with forms and enough questions you'd think they were digging for his life story.

"Oh boy . . ." his chapped lips let out a cheerless laugh when his eyes moved down the page to a blank space following the words "Emergency Contact."

His calloused fingers found their way into his flannel shirt pocket digging for cigarettes, but he stopped them when he realized what he was doing and instead let out a deep, tobacco-less sigh. His tired blue eyes found a spot on the ceiling while he mindlessly tugged at a messy white beard with one hand and tapped, tapped, tapped the office's cheap blue pen on the clipboard with the other, trying to think of what to scribble in the blanks. Phone number? Address?

He subconsciously stared at a fly trapped behind the plastic guard of the ceiling light. The insect crashed into the plastic again and again but kept going at the same pace, unfazed by its repeated failure to find an escape. Phantom wanted to stand on the chair to free the thing, but he stopped himself after taking a good look around the crowded room. His palms sweat and lungs tightened; everything about the place sent his heart racing. Bleached walls entrapped two dozen metal chairs stacked so close to one another Phantom could hear the pen of the guy next to him swoosh over his own stack of forms. It felt like the heat was set at ninety degrees, which only made the smell of retired people that much thicker. It all made him feel halfway around the world from where he wanted to be.

He took a deep breath in and released it slowly, hoping the frustration might follow the air out, a practice he adopted as a kid. He set his dusty cowboy hat on the chair next to him, let his balding head fall back to rest on the wall behind him, and closed his eyes.

A moment later, his eyes involuntarily returned to the ceiling to find that fly now lying lifeless on the clear plastic.

"You know what? Damn this whole thing," he thought. He stood up, flung his worn-out backpack over his shoulder, and threw the clipboard on the metal chair—the clank triggered every head in the room to bob up. "Sorry 'bout that," he mumbled as he darted past them.

His hiking boots carried him out the room and down a long hallway, the dingy carpet muffling each stomp toward the red exit sign, until half a foot from the glass door, they brought him to a halt.

Even from the cramped office, through the smudged fingerprints on the glass door, he could see the peaks of the Sierra Nevada Mountains that had drawn him in for as long as he could remember. Mount Tom stood taller than the rest and towered thousands of feet above the little town, making it look even more insignificant. The sun twinkled just beyond the peak as it set, as if it were a friend winking.

The old man slowly let in a lungful of air, impure compared to the crisp oxygen held on the other side of the glass. Then, he took off his cowboy hat and let his head drop to his chest in surrender.

Phantom would later call that moment his fork in the road. Standing there alone in that hallway, a stack of unanswered questions at one end and all the freedom of the High Sierra on the other, he struggled to convince himself to stay. Finally, whispering to no one, he said through clenched teeth, "S'pose it won't hurt to hand in what I got," and he turned around to march back to that metal chair.

He flipped through his forms one last time, like a kid giving a final glance over an exam, then handed them to a plump gal behind the desk. "Afternoon, ma'am. Here you go," he said, doing his best to deliver a cheerful sentence to make up for some of the questions he'd left blank.

She freed the papers from the clipboard and tossed them in a metal tray without looking down. "We'll call ya if we have questions," she snapped.

"Well, now, ma'am . . . I don't have a phone quite yet," his voice nearly drowned out by the "next" she hollered to the man behind him. Her eyes darted back to Phantom, "What . . . OK, just stop back in a week or so."

"How long you think it'll take to get everything processed?"

"I don't know, month or so," she said in more of a question than an answer, before grabbing a clipboard from the next person in line.

He put his cowboy hat in its place. After grumbling under his breath about the gal's rudeness to the gray-haired woman behind him, he started down the hall again toward the exit. His boots pounded the carpet in a slower gait this time, not yet ready to find out what now awaited him beyond the glass door. At least he'd done what he came to do.

He pushed through the heavy door to the parking lot and paused just long enough to grab a cigarette from his pocket and feel the jolt of February air cut through his bones. "Whoowie," he howled and gave his arms a rub to warm them back to life. It always felt ten times colder outside after getting a taste of warmth.

He walked to the rear of the office to pick up his mode of transportation—a Huffy mountain bike old enough to collect its own version of Social Security. He found it at a thrift shop a few years back when he was getting tired of walking into town and he'd since come to consider it more of a companion than a forty-pound hunk of metal. His favorite aspects of it were all the stuff that would deter even a kleptomaniac from giving it a second look. Its rusted joints made it creak with each pedal stroke; the tires were made up of more patches than rubber; the brake pads were a distant memory; and it gave off a stench of Sierra trout that he didn't seem to notice.

Creek-crack, creeek-craack . . . Phantom got his wheels rotating slowly toward his temporary home. He made a turn onto Main Street, and all of the little shops, diners, and motels that he used to frequent over the years came into view. It was like a framed picture of his past.

He looked over each of the shops lining the half-mile stretch of pavement. He used to duck into them every few months to make a few bucks, just enough to afford to return to his life in the wild. He had swept up popcorn at the old Bishop Twin Theatre. Painted the bright blue siding at Thunderbird Motel. Helped repair shelves at Joseph's Market. Worked on and off for two summers as a line cook at Jack's Restaurant, right next door to his go-to spot for fishing supplies, Mac's Sporting Goods. All of the shops looked as if they'd stood there as long as Mt. Whitney herself.

HE WASN'T IN THE MOOD to admit it on this evening, but Phantom thought, as far as towns went, Bishop was as good as it gets. People called it the gateway to the eastern Sierra Nevada Mountains. It was the final place to fuel up, get a bite to eat, and grab last-minute supplies before any excursion.

He thought of it as a city on the edge, with rich adventure on one side and, really, just a whole lot of emptiness on the other. Head in three of four directions, and you would run into towering pine trees, waterfalls, streams, and crystal clear lakes with wild flowers dotting their shores. "It's like a heavenly playground," Phantom beamed when he described the mountain range. But take 395 south, and you would witness how California earned its brand as the Golden State.

Golden has a nice ring to it, but all it really means is dry—parched. Most of the United States gets enough moisture to cover it with wild grass or some sort of natural weeds or trees, but California chooses her foliage sparingly. It's a land of dust, where ChapStick is just as vital as food and water, and Smokey Bear's fire safety sign always warns "HIGH." And a four-hour drive through the state's most desolate stretch of land is what all these determined tourists must endure to make it to the beauty beyond Bishop. Phantom always thought it a pretty crappy introduction to the Sierra Nevadas. Like a teen pop band opening for Johnny Cash. Guess some might argue it made the main attraction all the sweeter.

For a stretch of at least forty miles, the only sign of civilization is a place they call the airplane graveyard—dozens of retired jets sit as a practical mirage in a twenty-acre dump yard. Then the road carries vacationers past Owens Lake, the sight of which is enough to force anyone to think about the global water crisis. It's really just the dried-up remains of what was once a huge lake. Now, it's the nation's largest single source of dust pollution.

Soon they come across a sign inviting those ready to stretch their legs to see the empty shell of Manzanar War Relocation Center. Yes, the World War II Japanese internment camp. Only in the desert would that be an appreciated rest stop.

Eventually odd but welcomed buildings pop up out of nowhere. Trailer homes are lost among yards of tired vehicles, and a few restaurants manage to stay open to feed tourists whose hunger won't wait until Bishop. And then there's the Indian Wells Brewing Company, which seems as if it got lost on its way to a college town, gave up looking, and plopped down on the west side of 395.

Following each blip of a site that slips past is another stretch of flat, dusty California terrain that causes most tourists to think they must've missed a turn somewhere. Until, before they realize it, the two mountain ranges the highway split through the whole drive—the White Mountains to the east and the Sierra Nevada Mountains to the west—have met in the middle to deliver them to Bishop.

After a drive like that, the tired three thousand-person town suddenly looks like an oasis that no one is going to pass up.

THE HUFFY CREAK-CRACKED its way along Main to carry Sierra Phantom past the first stop that almost all tourists make as soon as they pull into town. You'd think it'd be a Wal-Mart so folks could stock up on supplies. Maybe a gas station after going so long without one in sight, or some great monument that explains the area's magnetic pull for vacationers. But it's a place that only provides something nobody really needs. It's a bakery. Erick Schat's Bakkerÿ.

A German family started the operation out of their home a hundred years ago, and now they're known all over the world for their sheepherder bread. People will delay their journey to some of the most beautiful mountain peaks and freshwater lakes on God's green earth to stand in line for forty-five minutes to buy a loaf of the stuff. They come out, eyes still glazed over from the drive, clenching white paper baggies brimming with bread, pastries, fudge, and any other treat that pertains to a vacationer's diet. On weekends, tour buses squeeze their way into the bakery's parking lot to unload skiers, hikers, fishermen, backpackers, and other adventuresome types.

And just as predictable as a line out the door on a Saturday morning was, for years, Sierra Phantom. As long as a weekend or a perfect summer day did its part to lure tourists, the mountaineer was there to greet them. At least a few times a month, he'd make his way down the mountain, settle into the same patio table, and peddle homemade fishing flies and stories that were just as colorful.

"Howdy," was always his line as patrons walked up, eyeing the flies he had laid out on the table. "What sort of adventure you on today?"

Most of the time they were either headed to Mammoth Mountain to ski, or they had that real tough angler twinkle in their eye that indicated they were craving a day with their line in one of the region's high elevation lakes. For those types, Phantom would let them in on some dynamite fishing spots, the backcountry waters that most don't know about.

"Well now, you got your Tioga Pass, the 20 Lakes Basin, and of course the Virginia Lakes. But the spot you'll probably most want to hit up is the Mammoth Lakes Basin . . ." Phantom recalled rattling this off to a young fisherman the previous summer who was visiting the High Sierra for the first time. "Now if you want to catch something special—I'm talkin' really something special—you want to head to Crystal Lake." He went on about what supplies to bring and what hiking trails would lead to the lake.

"And this special fish you're talking about?" the kid nudged.

"Oh, yes. I'm talkin' about the golden trout. You can only find these guys in a handful of waters, and they're finicky about what they'll eat. But, oh man, are they beautiful. I'll give ya one of these before you take off," Phantom said, pointing to a row of multi-colored flies hooked to his cowboy hat. "Fishin' these you're sure to snag a golden."

"Wow, all right, man. Thanks. That's where I'm headed."

"Now, bud, I have to tell ya: Don't be fishing there during the weekdays. You can keep your line in all weekend if ya want, but I like to keep these spots for myself during the week."

"Oh yes, sir. Of course," he straightened up and started in on his cinnamon roll. Then with a full mouth, he asked, "Guess you've spent some time up there, huh?"

"Some time?" He grinned through his beard and took off his cowboy hat so the kid could see his face worn from a life in the elements. "Man, I've lived up there since I was about your age."

"Really? Wow, sounds pretty cool. You got a cabin?"

"No. No cabin," he chuckled, "just me and the wilderness. I live off the land and move camps every few months so I don't leave a trace. And so the rangers don't catch up with me."

The guy's eyes doubled in size under his camouflaged baseball cap, the last of his roll sat in his mouth, which seemed to have forgotten how to chew.

"That's always been my home, and that's where I wanna die. Just me fallin' asleep under the stars," Phantom sat up straight and proud. And he made sure to add softly, "Don't really advertise this, son. Some folks here in town know that's how I live, but it's not really allowed, ya know?"

He knew he shared it too loudly and too often. He just loved seeing these city slickers' amazement when they heard that the mountains weren't a getaway after a workweek for him. They were his life, and they were the only life he wanted.

Phantom sighed as his Huffy carried him past the bakery, and his mind played back that conversation. That was almost eight months earlier, and already that life felt so far away. On this cold February evening, the bakery was quiet compared to the summer months; only a few kids in ski jackets made their way in and out of the double doors.

This town felt so different to him now, as if he were on the edge of it all looking in. He kept his wheels spinning past a row of the older motels—Creek Side Inn, Town House Motel, Elms Motel—then toward the end of the street to Bishop City Park. He looked right, then left and saw no cars coming, so he let the bike coast off the sidewalk into the park until the couple inches of snow brought it to a halt. He got off the now useless thing to push it the rest of the way. It creaked quietly and slowly, the only noise in the abandoned park. In the summer, you might see a family tossing a Frisbee around or a couple picnicking beneath the big, leafy trees. But it was empty and cold on this night. Its trees looked lifeless in their barren state, casting blue jagged shadows on the snow and doing little to block the breeze.

He stopped toward the back of the park and laid the bike on the snow. His hands reached in his pack for a baggie of almonds as he collapsed at the base of a large willow tree. He picked the side opposite the street in hopes no one would see an old mountaineer sleeping in a city park. Just didn't seem right.

He burned through a fresh cigarette, a welcome illusion of warmth, laid his head back on the willow's cold bark, and fell asleep.

CHAPTER

Post Front

*(n.) The period following a cold front;
the atmosphere clears and becomes bright.*

OVER THE NEXT EIGHT WEEKS, Sierra Phantom became a practical mascot at the Social Security office. He stopped in every day, half the time with a bribe in the form of a Schat's pastry for the blonde behind the counter until the two of them were on a first name basis.

"Howdy, Sue," he crooned one morning, still doing his best to suck up. "The man without so much as a receipt as record of his existence," she said flatly, not bothering to look up from her work. "What do you want now?"

"Oh, just keeping up my usual fight with Uncle Sam," he delivered the line with a plastic grin.

"Well, on that note, I have some news for ya," she said, still expressionless as she looked up at him.

"Really?" his voice cracked in surprise.

Without another word, she turned to a stack of white envelopes on the counter behind her and thumbed through them until she found the one she was looking for and presented it to him. Through the envelope's window he could see the name "John P. Glover."

He ripped open the envelope to find a check for $415. It was golden in color, complete with a picture of Lady Liberty and the words "United States Treasury" in big bold letters in the corner. It felt like the first gift he'd received from a cruel parent. But to Sue all he could say was, "How'd you do it?"

She shrugged and offered a half smile. "Now, let me get to these other people in line." There was the usual crowd camped out on metal chairs leaning over clipboards. "They'll mail ya a check on the third Wednesday of the month."

"Well, I'll just swing by to pick them up for a while," he said, not willing to let anyone know he was living more like a homeless man than a mountaineer. "We'll see ya next month, hon," he said as he put on his cowboy hat and turned toward the door.

"Actually, wait a minute," she hollered after him, "I got more news." Sue allowed herself a grin as if she'd been holding it in all day.

"Oh yeah, what's that? Sorry, excuse me . . ." He stepped back up to the counter despite the eye roll he got from an older woman next in line.

"I got you a place," she whispered.

"What?" he leaned in. "Wait, what do you mean?"

She handed him a folder of papers that advertised at the top "Valley Apartments: Senior Living Facility." The last three words made his face cringe as if he'd tasted something sour, but he quickly turned it into a smile.

Sue hadn't noticed. "It's just down Clarke Street. I think it used to be a motel in like the '40s or '50s, and then they turned it into affordable housing. They always have a waiting list, but I pulled some strings. Anyway, it's not great, but it's a place."

"Oh, hon, this is great," his smile stretched wider. "This is really great." He knew she'd hate him for it, but he ran around the end of the counter to give her a hug. She stood limp while the skinny old man almost picked her up off the ground.

"You can't be back here," she scolded.

He rambled on, "I mean, if I gotta live down here at least I can have some sorta home, ya know?"

"Seriously, Mr. Glover," she snapped.

"OK, OK . . . I gotta go get settled into my new place, anyway. We'll see ya."

DING, DING . . . He tapped the bell on the counter in the small office of Valley Apartments. "Hellooo, anybody here?"

The office door opened behind him, and a woman who looked just as tired as the apartment complex walked in. "Sorry about that," she said breathlessly, "I was changing a light bulb. What can I do for ya?"

"My name is Sierra Pha—well, it'd be under John P. Glover. I was told I got an apartment here."

"Oh yes, good to meet ya. I'm Elizabeth, manager of the place. Let's get you set up." She stepped behind the counter, opened a drawer, and dug around a few seconds until she pulled out a contract written up on a single sheet of paper. More blanks to fill in. "Read that over and sign down there. Let me know if you have questions."

Phantom took off his cowboy hat, nodded, and put on a nonchalant face as if he knew the answers to each of the questions. What he didn't know he made up, hoping it might at least buy him a few weeks of shelter while she fact-checked it all. He handed the form back to her with a casual grin. She put it in the drawer without giving it a glance and grabbed a single key that dangled from one of several hooks on the wall behind her. "All right, you're good to go. Number fourteen. Just across the way there."

The place looked just as you might imagine an old motel. Nothing worth including in a postcard home, but just enough to get a few hours of sleep between days full of Sierra fun. The eighteen rooms-turned-apartments wrapped around the paved lot in a U-shape. In the center was just enough room for a wooden awning, that not only offered shade for a small patio area but also a place to display three duct-taped signs that seem to scream, "NO PARKING!" At the entrance of the complex sat its best feature: a mammoth cottonwood with branches that reached clear from Apartment 1 to Apartment 18; it was the kind of tree worth mentioning in a home sale ad. But Phantom thought it somehow made the complex look even less significant.

He walked his bike across the lot to the door that was barely hanging onto a crooked "14," and he unlocked it. Without going inside, he let the door, with its chipped, tired green paint, swing open. He stood on the concrete just outside and surveyed the narrow space, all one room with white walls and beige carpet. In the back corner was an area they had made into a kitchenette of sorts, with an old oven and stovetop, a narrow refrigerator, and just enough counter space to prepare a fish dinner. In the city, they call these places studio apartments. Seemed too kind a name for Apartment 14.

The gratefulness of what the woman at the Social Security office did for him never wore off. But as his boots stood just shy of that beige carpet, all he could think about was falling asleep beneath the pine trees and breathing in the fresh scents of the High Sierra. He felt like turning around and running, fleeing right back to freedom. Before the thought could mature into action, he heard, "Just moving in?"

A woman smiled up at him from a chair outside the apartment next door. He hadn't noticed her sitting there. He turned his head toward her and forced a smile. "Yes, ma'am." Then he looked back at the one-room habitat and mumbled more to himself, "Just gettin' used to all this . . ."

"Well, I guess that makes us neighbors. I'm Carmen." She was a short, gray-haired woman with a kind, round face.

"Hi, Carmen," he said, taking off his cowboy hat and offering a handshake. "People call me Sierra Phantom."

"Well, that's a mouthful," she chuckled. "Yeah, s'pose it is," he offered a narrow grin.

"But I think I can handle it. You need help moving anything?"

"No, no. It shouldn't be too bad."

"Well, once you get settled, I can tell you what you need to know about this place."

"Alrighty, I'll take ya up on that," he nodded politely.

He had to think hard before he took his next step, as if his mind needed to override his body in order to step into the apartment. His dirt-caked hiking boots hit the carpet first, followed by his overloaded backpack. Then he pulled his Huffy in and set it against the wall before closing the door behind him.

He stood still, surveying what he could from just inside the front door for almost a full minute before finally exploring the place. He peeked into the bathroom, the only room separated from the rest of the apartment, then opened and closed the empty refrigerator and oven. Then he stood awhile longer so it would seem as if he had at least a bit of unpacking to do. He detached his fishing rod and his small briefcase full of fishing flies from his bike and set them in a corner.

"Unpacked," he joked aloud to himself.

He finally stepped outside and said to his new neighbor, "I think I'll take a little break."

While he settled into a second chair she'd pulled out from her apartment, she disappeared inside and returned with a mug of hot tea. "I realized after you went inside that I've seen you before," she said. "I've seen you in front of the bakery down on Main. Mostly in the summer months, I guess."

"Yes, ma'am. That's a good spot for me to sell my flies."

She didn't wait for an explanation before launching into an orientation of sorts of Bishop's Valley Apartments. As she went on about the variety of tenants, it was the sunset that held Phantom's attention. It glowed through the cottonwood branches until it finally slid behind Mount Tom. When it did, the mountaineer followed. He said goodnight and slipped back into the apartment to try out his first night of sleep under a roof in a long time.

CHAPTER

Catch and Release

(v.) A practice intended as a technique of conservation. After capture, the fish is returned to the water before serious injury.

SIERRA PHANTOM WOKE with the taste of carpet in his mouth. It was the burning smell of synthetic heat blasting through the vents that interrupted his night's sleep, a mere four-hour stretch of unconsciousness he'd spent sprawled out in the center of Apartment 14. He rubbed his eyes, dry from his artificial surroundings, and sat up straight.

He gave his beard a scratch as he came to, and then noticed the silence. It felt as if he'd woken up in a Tupperware. The feeling of a completely sealed room, void of any fresh air or nature's nighttime whispers suddenly made him aware of how alone he was. The green glow of the incorrect time on the microwave offered the closest resemblance of the familiar glimmer of the moon. He got to his feet, slid open the apartment's only window, and returned to lay on his back, looking up at the ceiling until he'd given up on sleep.

Just before dawn, he tucked a bandana full of silver dollar pancakes into his shirt pocket, perched a fishing rod over his shoulder, and began to pedal along the edge of 395 toward the mountains. This was how he'd planned to start most days now. It was as if a day back in the outdoors gave him a lungful of oxygen before he had to dive back down to the depths of humdrum townie life—paying rent, fetching dinner from a freezer, taking in the view of a parking lot out his window—and within twenty-four hours he would fight again to reach the surface to pull in another lifesaving breath.

His closest escape from Apartment 14 was Pleasant Valley Reservoir, the only body of water within twenty miles of Bishop. It didn't take a local expert to see that it certainly was not a naturally occurring body of water. It offered a rare flash of color on the northern edge of the valley, cutting through the dry basin's brittle desert shrubs and otherwise beige terrain. The barren nature of the place nudged tourists to move along up 395 toward the peaks and higher elevation lakes beyond it. In Phantom's former life, there was rarely a need to hike down to the reservoir except for an occasional visit to openwater fish in the winter. But now he welcomed it as his sanctuary away from town.

When he arrived at the water's edge, he detached a bright orange fly from his cowboy hat, tied it in its place and cast it as far as he could fling it. The moment the fly touched the water, Phantom felt content. Like breaking a massive pane of glass with a pin, it sent out a pattern of ripples, and he was home again.

He took in a whiff of the crisp spring air, the kind that still has an edge on it to let you know winter isn't far behind. His favorite season in the wild was always spring. In March or April he found himself appreciating things that might seem so drab at any other time: sixty-degree weather, wild berries for breakfast, and morning sunshine warming his face after a cold night's sleep.

He put out his usual cast and let the fly rest for half a second. Gave it a gentle tug. Then repeated the motion. The key was to make the fly look like an insect that fell into the water. A real bug would sit there for a second in shock and then start to try to swim its way out or attempt to fly away. Phantom always pictured it as though he were an actor on stage, playing a role to lure in the audience.

He gave it a tug, let it sit a second, and gave it another tug. At that, the fly disappeared, and the line went tense. "Alrighty, come on now . . ." he whispered to the fish as it considered the bait and finally gave in. As soon as the fish realized that it hadn't swallowed just any insect, it jerked its body right, then left. Phantom cranked the reel faster to keep it hooked. The thing kept up its fight to try to pull free from the line until it launched its whole body above the surface. Its blue-green scales with a pink streak along its side glistened in the morning sun.

"Whoowie, what a beauty. Come on now," the fisherman nudged as he towed the trout in with speed until he could lift it out of the water by the line. "Ah, there you are," he smiled, raising the fish to meet him at eye level. "Mornin', champ."

It was a decent-sized rainbow trout, so Phantom freed it from the hook and tossed it in his small cooler with a splash. "You'll be all right, bud. If I can find your bigger brother, you'll go scot-free."

His catches went on like that the rest of the day until his arms got tired from hauling them in. He set his net on a boulder to dry in the afternoon sun and took a seat among the rocks that were situated like a naturally made recliner. He unwrapped his pancakes and took a swig from his water bottle. "Now, this is living, huh?" he directed the words toward the cooler of fish.

He let in a deep breath, and as he released it, he noticed he had no urge to reach in his shirt pocket for smokes. They never came to mind while he was sitting along the water's edge. He felt no stress, no meaningless compulsions. Not out here.

After perfect days on the water, it was the draw of the wild that returned stronger than ever. Seeing the peaks just beyond the reservoir, he felt tempted to retreat deep into the forest to cook up dinner over a fire like he used to, then fall asleep counting the stars.

The awesomeness of the High Sierra, her wonder, her dangers, was a savory addiction all its own. For as long as he could remember, Phantom felt as if he couldn't escape her, and he didn't want to. Even if he were gone a few days to restock supplies, he felt it was too long. He imagined it might be like that for a young guy in love. He'd rather not experience even hours apart from her if he could help it.

Of course, when his temptation for a life in some of the continent's wildest terrain got the best of him, his string of memories conveniently excluded frostbite and avalanches and the pure exhaustion of working for everything a body and mind needs to survive. Up there, water, protection, food, and shelter only come with effort, and a lot of it. He never liked to admit it, but keeping himself alive during the coldest months had become a real challenge in his final years in the wild.

He took a bite of his lunch as he looked up toward the rocky mountain range from the reservoir's shore, and let his thoughts wander back to that January morning, the day he could no longer stay ahead of what Mother Nature was dishing out, the day he thought would be his last.

Two months earlier, High Sierra

HE KNEW SOMETHING WAS COMING. He was taught in the Navy how to predict the weather, and white, wispy clouds and a breeze with a cold bite late that morning told him a cool spell was on its way. Storms in the High Sierra can dump more than two feet of snow in less than twenty-four hours, and Phantom knew that they could strand him for days. He needed to prepare for the worst.

As much as weather occupied his thoughts in the coldest months, it was the effort to get enough fat to keep him from starving and freezing that demanded most of his energy. Trout don't have much fat on them, so he had to make up for it in other ways. On occasion, he'd hunt for deer. He could get between twenty and twenty-five pounds of fat from a doe, and he'd slide a tablespoon of that into everything he ate; he even dropped a dollop in his coffee each morning. And as backup, he kept a stash of candy bars for a quick boost of energy. But on that day, even his Hershey bars were gone, so he set out to gather what he could from his traps.

As he hiked near the shadow of Mount Humphreys he could feel the temperature drop lower every few minutes. He kept on, though. He had convinced himself he needed to get food to last him through the storm. He hiked two or three miles until he reached a trap he'd set up days before. It sat wide open just as he'd left it, still holding its pecan. He put the nut in his pocket and hiked to a second trap. He found it, ten paces off a little frozen pond, clamped shut. The nut nowhere to be found.

"Damn," he lamented, "thing got away."

Now he was growing concerned about what the next forty-eight hours held. It was too late to drill a hole in the ice to catch anything. He'd probably get trapped right in the middle of the storm at this point. He started talking to himself, mumbling, "If this snowstorm holds off, best case, I'll just go to sleep hungry. First thing tomorrow I'll hike down and restock. And worse case . . ." His mind raced trying to think of his options. He hadn't seen a deer or much life to speak of for days. Everything was in hiding. It was just too damn cold.

The temperature had to be at least ten degrees below zero, and there he stood a couple of miles from his camp. He convinced himself to start hiking back the same way he had come. He pulled a compass from his pack, and began to move in the direction the red arrow pointed. He marched through the few inches of snow that had fallen days before. On the way out, the snow crunched beneath his boots but didn't hold him up a second. Now it felt as if it was grabbing hold of his feet with each step. First the right, and he'd pull it free, then the left. The bitter cold has a way of slowing things down. He felt like he was swimming in molasses. He moved slower and slower and grew weaker.

His toes and fingers had gone from feeling numb to feeling on fire, like a thousand needles were pressing through his chapped skin. He gave one last push to walk another few feet until he convinced himself that a moment's rest would renew his energy to keep going, and then he collapsed in exhaustion. He stared blankly at the clear blue sky above him, as his mind went in and out like a bad cable connection. He let his eyes fall and listened to his lungs suck in and then push out air slower and slower until they nearly gave up.

He didn't know how long he was unconscious, but he woke with a jolt. His eyes shot open when he heard, "Sierra Phantom! Phantom . . ." It was the familiar voice of an old friend. It was Sanuye, his eyes blazing with a fear Phantom had never seen in him. He gripped the mountaineer's shoulders and shook him back to life.

Sanuye was a Paiute Indian. Phantom first met him when he was new to the wilderness lifestyle and needed warm clothes for the winter. He brought Sanuye and his tribe fish and venison, and they gave him pelts in return.

"Phantom, let's go. You need to get warm," Sanuye said, bending his knees as if he was ready to pick him up.

"No, no," he whispered, brushing Sanuye's helpful hands away. He felt OK to let go. He'd lived the last fifty years of his life just how he wanted to. And if there was anything he knew for certain, it was that he didn't want to die in a stuffy house, or worse, some sterile old folks' home. There was something beautiful and simple about falling asleep beneath Sierra's peaks, buried by the snow that had kept him on his toes all these years. "This is my exit," he thought to himself.

"If nature . . ." he started, weakly, ". . . wants to take me . . . let her." His eyelids fell again.

"Sierra Phantom," Sanuye hissed the words in insistence. "You can't just give up like this. Think of what you've learned about nature, preservation, about survival. You can't let all of that knowledge, all those experiences just die."

At those cruel words, the mountaineer opened his eyes. He could make out a tear rolling over the Indian's withered face. His brown eyes looked into Phantom's in insistence, as if he knew something Phantom didn't. Too weak to argue, the mountaineer lifted his arm and let Sanuye gently hoist his feeble frame over his shoulder.

The next thing he remembered was waking to a light so bright it made his eyes sore. For just a fleeting moment, he thought it might be that radiance people who've lived through near-death experiences talk about, described like a beacon summoning them from the other shore. He blinked hard, and blinked again, until his mind caught up to reality and brought into view the cheap fluorescent ceiling lights of the Northern Inyo Hospital Emergency Room in Bishop. Just as soon as the patient had come to grips with where he was, a balding, middle-aged man appeared in the foreground wearing a white coat, a stethoscope and a disapproving scowl.

If the doctor offered a "good morning" or a "how you feeling," Phantom couldn't recall it. The first words that his mind bothered to hang on to were a cruel message that had him hoping it was just a dream. Over the persistent beep of a heart monitor, the doctor went on about hypothermia, pneumonia, and frostbite. "You're not gonna make it another month, even another day, up there. Not at your age," he scolded.

The warning sent a jolt of anger, or maybe it was fear, from Phantom's gut to the top of his head. He bit his lip and swallowed to keep the feeling from escaping in the form of a scream or a smack right on the doctor's cheek. Convinced that the doctor would report him to the game wardens if he publicized his plans to walk right out of the hospital's glass doors and return to his life at ten thousand feet, he instead targeted what little energy he had to a grin.

"Doc," he said, his voice as loud as his strength would allow, though still little more than a whisper, "you know what they say, 'You can take the man outta the wild, but you can't take the wild outta the man.'"

Those words, although laced with a fake smile, were the truest the mountaineer had ever spoken.

CHAPTER

Blind Cast

(v.) Casting at no particular target.

"OFF YOU GO," Phantom instructed the first rainbow trout he'd caught at the reservoir earlier that morning. A larger brown trout he snagged later in the day bought the rainbow's freedom. The fisherman set the rainbow back in the reservoir, but the stunned creature stayed still. Thinking he was still trapped in a Styrofoam cooler, he helplessly bobbed along with the gentle current that flowed between the rocks near the shoreline. "You're home," Phantom promised and gently nudged the fish with his hand. Then, finally convinced, it took off like a bullet.

The fisherman smiled and gave one last satisfying look at the water before gathering his gear. Just as the sun was set to slide behind Mount Tom for the day, he began his coast back to town.

He turned the Huffy onto Highway 395 and worked to hold his focus on the mountains on the opposite side of the valley, the slick rock faces of the White Mountains glowed an orange-pink reflection from the sun setting behind him. He picked up his speed, telling himself it was because in five minutes the color show would be over and night was waiting to take its turn. But really, he was struggling to outpedal an unsettling thought, as if it couldn't touch him within Bishop city limits.

His legs took turns pushing with all their strength until the Huffy felt as if it were going to take flight. Instead it carried him along the highway's smooth pavement toward the dim lights of Main Street, which his eyes honed in on like a gunman approaching a target. He tried to distract himself with thoughts of how he might fix his fish dinner, then whether tomorrow held another day on the water or maybe an afternoon selling flies in front of the bakery. His every attempt to focus on something else, anything else, was taken over by the raspy, tired voice of his friend. He shook his head in an empty attempt to rattle the Indian's words out of him and spun his pedals faster still.

He couldn't shake them. His legs kept the pedals spinning, but something inside of him kept asking, "What am I supposed to do now? Why didn't Sanuye just let me go?" His thoughts, now out of his control, settled on an admission he wasn't ready to make. What was the goddamn point of living up there all those years, or living at all, if he just disappeared without a trace? At that, the Huffy skidded off the road, and he hit the hand brakes to jolt himself to a stop.

"Damn . . . !" His shout disappeared in to the valley's abyss. He sucked in the desert's dry air and coughed it back out. He threw the Huffy to the ground and paced beside the quiet highway, letting the nagging thought hang there alongside the cloud of kicked-up dust. He finally bent over to rest his hands on his knees and pulled in deep breaths.

As the dust and his breathing both finally settled, he guided his steps back to the bike. His boots found the pedals again and did their part to get the wheels rotating toward Apartment 14. He let them carry him now at their own unrushed pace, as if he'd surrendered control over them right along with everything else.

It was a weekday between tourist seasons, so it felt like the Bishop that Phantom had first become acquainted with more than fifty years earlier. The Huffy's slow creak-crack seemed like the only sound for miles. Several vacant signs glowed red above motels, and the popular Giggle Springs Gasoline Market, known to sell the cheapest gas for   a hundred miles, sat empty except for a bored high school kid manning the register. The diner's fluorescent lights shone through big pane windows onto the street. Phantom peeked in on his way past; just a few locals occupied the booths. His bike coasted by the rest of Main Street's offerings, Union Bank of California, Anne Marie's, Sierra Office Supply, Taylor's Family Shoes, all of which sat mostly empty and quiet as if taking a rest until the vacationers returned. And then something made him screech the Huffy's wheels to a halt. That lone sound in town that night bounced off the buildings that crowded either side of the narrow street.

He turned his head back to Sierra Office Supply and looked up toward the faded blue and red letters. His warm breath floated in a cloud toward the sign's subhead: Xerox Copy Center. "Well, might as well set this thing into motion," he thought aloud. As if he'd made a New Year's resolution he didn't want to wear off, he got off his bike, rested it on the side of the building, and pulled open the glass door to the shop.

"Welcome to Sierra Office Supply," a young woman behind the register mumbled without looking up from a magazine.

"Howdy ma'am. How are ya?" Phantom offered, trying to yank her eyes up from the page with no luck. He paused a moment, hoping the awkward silence would kick her customer service skills into gear. No luck.

"Well, let me just show ya what I'm lookin' for this evening." He set his cowboy hat on the counter, plucked a pencil from a bouquet of them jammed in a coffee mug, and pulled out a little notebook from his backpack. "SIERRA PHANTOM" he etched in big letters at the top and then in smaller letters below it, "Creator of the Glitter Flies – Fishing Guide to the Eastern High Sierra Lakes $50 Per Person Per Day."

"Could you print this up on two hundred or so business cards?"

Her narrow hazel eyes now studied the feathers and fishing flies superglued to his cowboy hat. "Where you from? I'll betcha not LA, maybe Denver?"

"Well, actually, I lived part of my childhood in LA. But most my life I spent in the High Sierra. I learned a lot out there, and I figure I should pass some of that on to the younger generation. Make sure they preserve it, ya know?" The words sputtered out of him at record speed.

When he first made his home in the mountains, he felt like a pioneer discovering one of the best-kept secrets west of the Missouri. Although he had never owned a foot of land in his life, he somehow felt a sense of ownership for the entire mountain range.

"So, that's what I'm doing here," he told the girl. "I want to operate sort of my own, one-man guide business."

"Hmm," she said, sounding as if she wished she hadn't asked. She held up the sheet of paper and took a long look at what he'd scribbled.

Then, she looked her customer over one last time before announcing, "I can have these ready for you first thing tomorrow."

"That's perfect. Thank you, darlin'," he said. He started toward the door but stopped when he noticed the girl walk to the back of the shop, where computers and large printers hummed.

"You printing these now?" he yelled after her. When she nodded, he said, "I'll just hang tight 'til you're through."

"Suit yourself."

Within an hour, he had a stack of his very own business cards in hand. When he got back to the apartment, he threw the fish in the fridge and got to work on a thorough promotional plan for his new enterprise.

He emptied his tackle box of paints that gave the glitter flies their name and aligned each eight-ounce bottle on the counter: pink, green, gold, blue, yellow . . . enough colors to outshine a rainbow trout. On the brim of his cowboy hat, he wrote in green: "Pro Mountaineer + Fishing Guide." He moved onto his snap-button shirts and wrote "Sierra Phantom" over one shirt pocket and "Pro Mountaineer" over the other. Then he grabbed the gold glue to write a résumé of sorts on the back of the shirts: "Pro Mountaineer + Fishing Guide (1946), Creator of Glitter Flies (1956)."

He held the first completed shirt up toward the ceiling light and smiled. "Not bad. Not bad at all." And then he rewarded himself with a smoke.

By the time the sun was ready to usher in the day, almost every stitch of clothing he owned let people know what he was selling. Just as he convinced himself he'd better get a few minutes of sleep, he put the same type of calligraphy on his fake leather briefcase that carried his flies: "Ask About Guided Tours." Before letting the paint dry, he hung the briefcase in its place on the top tube of the Huffy and fell back on his thrift store couch in satisfaction.

"Well, lookie there," smoke escaped from his smile. "Open for business."

SIERRA PHANTOM WOKE WITH A JOLT just after 8:00 a.m. It took him a second to remember what project he'd been working on. Shirts and jackets and hats covered every bit of the living room floor he wasn't occupying. He shook his head to wake everything up and told himself he had to get moving if he wanted to catch the morning crowd.

He allowed one big stretch and then jumped to his feet to kick the day into high gear. Running around the apartment in just long johns and a cowboy hat, he dug through a bag of his recent thrift store purchases to pull out a fresh pair of Wranglers. He yanked them on and grabbed one of his favorite flannel shirts, now a bit flashier than the day before, and made his way to Schat's.

The bakery was the perfect place to kick off his guide business. He and Erick, the owner, had become buddies years earlier when Phantom was looking for a place to sell glitter flies. "People love seeing a genuine outdoorsman just as they're starting their own Sierra adventure," Erick had always told him.

But Erick Schat certainly didn't need the help of a mountaineer mascot to turn a profit. He had his staff churning out 25,000 loaves of bread each week and 450 different products each day to keep up with demand. And he set up the bakery so customers had to walk past every single one of those treats before they reached the register. Phantom thought the winding aisles stacked tall with goodies looked like a cattle shoot for tourists. It was a sweet tooth's paradise and a claustrophobic's worst nightmare.

He was friends with most the workers, so they let him sneak past customers waiting in the shoot. "Howdy, boys," he announced when he reached the counter on this particular morning. One was pulling a tray of cookies out of their titanic oven while the other fetched a woman coffee. "Phantom, how are ya? It's been a while," one guy shouted from the register as he gave a customer change. "What ya been up to?"

He had avoided any of his regular spots while he was getting situated in town. He wasn't in the mood to chat, and he especially wasn't keen on anyone knowing he spent half the winter sleeping in the city park. "Oh, you know, just fishing every chance I get. I pulled a brown trout out of the reservoir yesterday."

"That right? Nice." He pulled a paper cup from a stack of them on the counter and filled it with coffee. Phantom set two dollars on the counter, but the cashier didn't touch it. "Coffee's always on the house for you. You know that."

"Alrighty, well, I'll get to it then. Thank you." He put his hat in its place and turned on his heel toward the door.

Phantom situated himself at his usual wobbly table out front. He set his briefcase open on the table to display his flies, next to a stack of his fresh-off-the-press business cards. Just as his teeth sank into that first warm donut, a line of vehicles, led by an old rumbling truck as blue as a robin's egg, snaked its way into the lot.

A few kids blasted around the corner in a race to the front door. The littlest boy reached it first and pulled the heavy wooden door open with all his might. He stood with his back against the door and feet stretched out on the concrete to keep it from closing in on him, and put on a proud grin as his older brother and sister and father walked through the doorway. "Why thank you, Luke," the father said, freeing him from his post. "Now, let's get that donut."

Phantom loved peoplewatching. Everyone was checking off their own sort of agenda for the day. He could spot the locals a mile away because they looked worn and generally less excited about everything; the desert can do that to a person. It was the tourists who were the most fun to watch. They were wrapping up a week of exhaustive fun, just making one last stop at the bakery on their way home. Or Schat's was the first taste of their Sierra getaway, as if a sugary pastry or a cup of coffee was fuel for their climb up Red Dihedral or their descent through Mammoth Mountain's powder.

He knew he didn't quite fit in with any of it. He certainly was no tourist. If he was, he was one of Sierra's first. You'd think he'd be considered a local because he'd lived in the area for so long, but locals didn't claim him. The criterion was strict to be considered a local. Seems you had to be of the same pedigree, born and raised there, and a third or fourth generation Bishopite to earn the brand. Then there were the people who made their way up the mountain from Southern California. Even if they'd been in town a decade or more, the locals didn't count them as one of their own. They called them flatlanders. And Phantom certainly didn't think he fell in to that category. He figured he was on the edge of it all, looking in.

"Good morning." The woman who was just barely peeking over the steering wheel of that blue pickup came around the corner. She beat Phantom to the greeting in a soft voice, holding her pace toward the front door. He didn't know her name, but he recognized her as a Schat's regular. She walked steadily but slowly with a cane in her right hand. She looked twenty years too young for it, but her measured steps indicated she must have been in some sort of pain.

Phantom abandoned his donut and jumped up to open the door for her. "Morning, hon. Gorgeous day, isn't it?"

"Yes, it certainly is," she smiled.

He made himself wait until she got her breakfast to give her his spiel. In the meantime, he unloaded what looked like a kid's art kit from his briefcase and got to work on his first fly of the day. He dotted super glue onto a shank hook and pressed a small bit of feather in place, then wrapped it all in an olive green thread. Between tying, he looked up to wave at cars lined up in the median of Main Street waiting to pull into the bakery. Suddenly it felt as if he was getting back to his old routine, or at least part of it.

The owner of the blue pickup came out a few minutes later with a small coffee in her hands. "Hey, hon . . ." Phantom looked up from his project. "Do you know anyone who would like a guided fishing trip or maybe a hike led by a real mountaineer?"

She paused in front of his table. "Hmm . . . well, my son's friends really love fishing. But I'm not much of a fisherman."

"Well, here's my card. You can tell them where to find me."

"I will. Thank you." She smiled and continued toward her truck.

As foot traffic picked up, Phantom gave a business card to anyone who would take one, and by the end of the day, he was a quarter of the way through his stack of two hundred. "I'll give you a great deal," he'd go on, "just fifty dollars, and I'll take you to see parts of the High Sierra you never knew existed. You know where to find me."

It took a couple of weeks for his self-promotion to return any business. But when word spread that the old man in front of Schat's did more than just smile and tie flies, he had more business than he could keep up with.

CHAPTER

The Hook

(n.) In journalism, the part of the article meant to catch readers' attention.

Present day, Northern Virginia.

MY BARE FEET PACED the creaky wooden floor of my bedroom as I dialed his number. With the first ring, I pulled the phone away from my ear ready to hang up, but I stopped myself. Ring . . . I half hoped it would go to voicemail. That would end this whole thing before it started. Ring . . . I'll give it two more rings, I made myself promise. I don't have time for something like this. Ring . . .

"Hello, Phantom here." The pacing stopped. My eyes darted around the room for my laptop, a notebook, anything to write on.

"Hello there?" The kind voice tried again. Each time, his hello emphasized the friendliest part of the word with a long o. "Hello?"

"Hello, sir," I finally started. My lips couldn't muster his name. "Yes, hello. This is Sierra Phantom," he spoke his superhero-sounding title just as casually as a man would say, "Tom Jones."

I didn't know where to begin. I'm not usually one to be nervous about cold-calling people. Ten years as a journalist and you'd better be over talking to strangers. Most newspaper editors make sure to knock any fear out of you before you're ever formally on the payroll.

As the moment hung there for far too long, I thought back to the first assignment I got as a summer intern. It's the first assignment of almost every intern: the "Man on the Street" column, which required wide-eyed journalism majors to walk up to four random people and ask their opinion about, say, gun control or the local election. Their answers ran on the Opinion page next to irate letters to the editor. But I swear it was less of a column for readers to enjoy and more of a training tool to give cub reporters a baptism by fire experience.

I've logged my share of "Man on the Street" assignments, so a phone call to a retired mountaineer shouldn't give me a second thought. But my usual spiel—introduce myself as a reporter with the So-and-So Post, cite the article I'm working on, explain how I'd like to include their perspective—didn't fit here. This felt too big for a spiel.

"Hi, Mr. Phantom. Um, this is Danielle. Calling from Virginia. My friend Craig, skinny Scottish guy you met at South Lake a few weeks ago, told me about you," my shaky voice successfully delivered the lines. "He said you might be interested in telling me your story. To possibly write a book on your experiences." Each statement sounded more like a question in search of an answer.

"Oh, yes. Howdy! He mentioned you might be callin'. How you doing, hon?" His words seemed to smile through the phone.

"Pretty good." I let my shoulders relax a bit before I continued trudging through my intro. "I just thought I'd give you a call to see if I could hear a bit of your story. Since we can't exactly sit down for a coffee, I thought we might just talk by phone. Is now a good time?"

"Sure, I'm just coming in from giving an allday tour up near Mosquito Flat. I started my own guide business . . ." As he spoke, I ran to the living room to find my laptop. "I spend almost every day outdoors. I hate bein' cooped up in this apartment, so if you wanna catch me, don't call in the middle of the day. Any time at night or real early in the morning though, I'm here."

You could hear his stubborn energy through the phone. His voice was deep, the kind of sound you might imagine coming from a man who preferred life in the elements. But his tone lifted slightly every few sentences, just enough to ward off any intimidation his words might carry. He didn't allow syllables or words or sentences to sit long. It made me think of one of my college professors who consistently tried to squeeze a two-hour lesson into a thirty-minute lecture.

"I've got a lot to share," the mountaineer said, explaining his rapid pace. "Why don't I give you an overview of my experiences and then see where we go from there. That sound good?"

"Yes, sounds great."

I plugged my laptop cord into the wall and took a seat at the kitchen table, poised to type. "Real quick, sir, can I get a couple of details out of the way?"

"Sure thing, hon."

"OK, first, what name do you prefer?" I felt the need to hear him confirm this bit of information.

"Sierra Phantom, or just Phantom's fine. Either way. I started out as John P. Glover, never known what the P stands for. I went by J.P. for a while, then just Glover, and when I was old enough to come up with something better, I did."

I laughed a little. "Sierra Phantom does have a nice ring to it. Now, how old are you?"

"I was born July 20, 1926, in Orange, California. Now I live in a little mountain town called Bishop."

I did the rough math in my head and realized he was about twenty years older than he sounded.

"Now, why don't I get to the good stuff?" He was like a rodeo bronco waiting for the gate to swing open. "I'll tell ya, I never imagined I would be living in a town surrounded by a bunch of people, falling asleep each night between the walls of an apartment."

"Go ahead." I secured my phone between my cheek and shoulder and began to type: Sierra Phantom, Bishop, Calif . . .

He cleared his throat with purpose and took a deep breath. "I'm a mountaineer, been that way most my life. I made my home in the High Sierra when I was in my early twenties. I set up eight camps from Mosquito Flat to South Lake, and I built each of these different depending on the season. In the warmer months, I'd build a simple lean-to with a very basic roof made of crisscrossed pine boughs. In the winter, I dug out a snow pit, like an igloo, about seven feet in diameter. 'Course, I always carried a sleeping bag for warmth. After a while at one camp, I'd put everything back as I found it and move to the next. This preserved the natural ecology and kept rangers from tracking me down. . ." His words came out smooth and fast as if he had spoken them all a hundred times before. "I had to trap, hunt, fish, gather wild greens, and use what was in the area, and every few months I'd go into one of these little mountain towns to stock up on supplies. I did just fine for more than fifty years up there. . ."

He paused, and then started again. "Well, until last winter when a real bad storm came in. I got hypothermia, pneumonia, and frost bite. I thought I'd die up there, but an Indian friend of mine, who I'd trade pelts with on occasion, found me and dragged me down to Bishop. Told me he wouldn't let me die up there alone and said I got a story worth telling. So here I am, now living in Bishop."

"So what made you decide to live up there in the first place?" I squeezed in the question as soon as he took a breath.

"Well . . ." he paused again. I heard a click, click, click as if he was lighting a cigarette. "I grew up as a ward of the state. I lived in four orphanages and three foster homes in fourteen years, raised by drunks and people who were just in it for a paycheck . . ." As the subject changed, his diction quickened, and his tone hardened. "So I learned early on in life how to survive on my own. I ran away from two of the places, but they found me and brought me back."

He stopped long enough to take a pull from his cigarette, so I chimed in. "So, is that what encouraged you to live out in the wild?"

"Sorta. I finally got sick of it all, of society in general. I didn't want a thing to do with any of it." He must've thought he was sharing too much because he suddenly snapped, "Anyway, 'nough about that."

"Darn it," I thought and shook my head. I'd spooked him. Too quickly I asked the question that, I would later learn, had come to define him

Journalism Rule #1: build a rapport with your source.

As if he were moving the needle on a record player, Phantom moved the conversation to the part of his life he enjoyed talking about. "But I survived just over fifty years up there. Taking everything Mother Nature throws at you and coming out on the other side, well, that's more gratifying than anything else this world can offer. I promise you that. You probably won't hear it from anyone else 'cause most haven't lived it to know. Nobody has made it that long in the High Sierra like that. And it wasn't easy like it is now. The winters before 1984 would last ten months out of the year . . ."

He told story after story: of surviving torrential downpours, making his own snowshoes, ice skating on the mountain lakes, and even something about inventing some fly-fishing lure that fetched him seventy-six fish on the first try. He seemed to be good at everything—carpentry, gardening, hunting, even painting—and he was the star of each of his stories. But something about the way he told them made me like him even more. He wasn't arrogant, but instead he was sweet in the way he spoke. As if he was inviting me to take a peek into his world of big adventures in which he was the tour guide.

". . . I dealt with dehydration, frost bite, hypothermia. You name it. But even with all that, if I had a choice, I'd live it all again in a minute."

"Really? Wow . . . So you ever get lonely up there?" As soon as the words left my lips, I realized I had done it again. I had a feeling the part of his story he was brushing over was what I most needed to know, and I knew that asking about it right out of the gate would probably finish this thing before it got started. "What I mean is—"

"Hell no," he loudly interjected, as bluntly as I'd asked the question. "For crying out loud, Mother Nature was my family. Living up there was the first time I really felt happy. There was just so much comfort out there . . ." his tone softened, and I sighed in relief while my fingers flew over my keyboard. "Even as a kid, I'd run away and hike five, ten miles without a compass and not even get lost. Even if I was gone a coupla days, it was like Mother Nature welcomed me back sayin', 'It's about time you got your ass back here.'"

I laughed, and he joined me.

"Wow," was all I could think to say. I had a mental list of subjects I wanted to ask him more about and an even longer list of items to fact check, but I stopped myself. "Ease into it," I told myself.

"Oh, you just wait, hon," he almost shouted the words. "This is just the tip of the iceberg."

CHAPTER

Source

(n.) A person or document that provides information.

(n.) A spring or fountainhead from which a river or stream issues.

NOTHING ABOUT WHAT WE WERE DOING was routine, but we did our best to make it feel that way. I'd call him on Sundays about 9:30 p.m. my time, 6:30 p.m. his time. If I called any earlier, all I'd get was his voicemail. "Sorry to miss ya. I'm probably out fishin'. Leave a message."

While my husband cleaned up dinner or folded the last of the week's laundry, I sat at my laptop with my phone pinned between my ear and shoulder, unsure what I would do with this gem of a tale but selfishly excited to get the leading character on the phone so I could hear more. And each time, with as little as a deep breath, he returned to his story.

The detail, the singsong intonation he provided each sentence transported us—him from a stale apartment, me from my kitchen table—to California 1930, Washington 1940, Alaska 1943, or wherever he'd left us the last time we talked.

In one of our first phone calls, I asked him to please start with his earliest memory. I knew he wanted to just "get to the good stuff," as he'd put it, about his years in the wild, but there was no sense for me to hear all that without knowing what chased him out there in the first place. I knew I couldn't put it to him that way. Instead I told him, "I can process this better in chronological order."

I expected his earliest memories would be of him at five or six years old—the Halloween when I was the only kindergartener to show up without a costume is about as far back as I can remember—but he promptly let me know his memory starts years earlier.

"My memory has always been crystal clear. So clear that it's like I can still physically feel even my earliest experiences. I swear to ya, I can remember the taste of fresh strawberries that I snatched from the kitchen when I was real little, like three or four years old. I can remember the feelings of textures, like the weight of my leather shoes passed down to me from one of the older boys and the fur of the neighbor's dog on my hands, as if I were experiencing it at this very moment. It's amazing what our minds retain," he said as if I, too, was taking that moment to recall such detailed encounters with strawberries and puppies.

"I honestly can't remember much before I was five or six," I admitted softly.

"Well, my first memory is as real as the day it happened," he continued. I heard the click of a cigarette lighter, and he paused a moment probably to take a drag. I got comfortable with my own vice, a mug of dark roast coffee. "I must've been three or so 'cause it was one of my first nights at my first orphanage, the Waverly Baby Home in Los Angeles. And it was my first attempt at an escape.

"I was lying in one of a dozen cribs that lined a long room. I'm sure I was scared or cold or hungry or somethin' because I remember desperately wantin' to get out of that crib. I fussed some, waiting for the sound of footsteps to click in my direction to comfort me, but they never came. I kicked a blanket off and worked my way to my feet. I remember grabbing the crib's bars and darting glances around the room like I was a little prisoner in a cell." He let out a laugh, picturing a sly little boy plotting his escape. "I got the blanket gathered in the corner of the crib, set a foot on the blanket, and pulled myself over the rail. And WAM!" He clapped his hands for effect. "My right cheek smacked the floor, and I let out a whimper. That prompted two nuns to blast through the doorway.

"'Oh, you boy,' one nun scolded, rushin' toward me.

"I took off, running as fast as my little legs would take me. The two nuns pulled their robes to their knees and slammed into one another just as they were gainin' on me. Their fumbling bought me time—I ducked under cribs and darted toward an open door and into a dark bathroom. I started crawling under the sink just as I heard, and felt, something smash to the floor. I had slammed into a glass jar of Purex. That loud crack of breaking glass startled me and brought me to tears, and my hiding spot was made public. One of the nuns, a real mean one, marched over. 'What have you done now, boy?'" Phantom delivered the line in a bossy squeal.

"She picked me up from the pile of glass by my underarms. Blood dripped from my sliced knee down my leg to the bathroom tile. I still have that scar on my knee all these years later." He paused a moment to catch his breath before adding, "You want another memory?"

"Of course," I smiled, took a sip of coffee, and kept typing.

"OK now, there were plenty of other escapes . . ." He trailed off in a thought he must've decided not to pursue. "I also remember learning to tie those heavy leather shoes that were handed down to me. Guess I was about five years old. I was at St. Agnes at that point."

I jotted down the second orphanage name on a notepad to help me keep them straight.

"The bigger kids seemed to whip the two laces into a perfect bow just as easily as they shoveled down their supper. At that point I'd give anything a shot if it meant I could avoid gettin' picked on. 'I gotta be able to do more stuff without their help,' I remember thinkin'. Tyin' my shoes might do. When I found a minute to myself, I plopped down on the back porch steps of the orphanage and got to work. As I slumped over my project, groups of boys marched passed between chores and run-ins with the headmaster, no doubt. A few took the time to knock me over or crack a joke as they past. Not one bothered to help me. But I swore to myself I didn't need their help. It took me almost an hour, but I finally cracked the code."

He laughed quietly, as though he was right back there. "I'm sure the loops were a bit lopsided, but I certainly stood a little taller that day.

"I also learned to sew at that same orphanage," he kept on without pausing. "Not because I had any desire to learn," he said with a bit of a snort. "It was part of my punishment."

"Punishment?" I asked.

"Oh yeah. There was a lot of that there. This one came after a fight over a swing. There was a real nice tire swing that hung from a big cottonwood tree next to the dormitory that I never got to swing on because the older kids always got to it first. Well, one day I finished mopping the floors early—we all had a list of chores to do every day—so I ran as fast as I could to the tree to swing before anyone else got to it. And I'll tell ya, just as I grabbed the rope, a girl about my age but twice my size pulled the swing out of my grip and hopped on."

"Ah man," I added.

"She giggled; she was so excited to steal it from me. She pushed the swing back with her feet and swooped forward with her pink tongue leadin' the way. I was so mad, I bolted toward her ready to rip out that tongue or that blonde hair, whichever I could reach first. Instead, I caught her jacket and ripped off one of the buttons. And of course she cried and told the headmistress.

"The headmistress yelled at me, 'You ain't gettin' nothing to eat 'til you sew that button back on.'" He sounded like he was impersonating an old witch. "She pushed me into a wooden chair; handed me the button, needle, and thread; and flopped the jacket on my lap. 'I'll let the cafeteria know you won't be making it to dinner.'

"Well, I'll tell ya now, I made it to dinner that night. A little late, but I made it. Took me hours to figure that thing out, especially with my small hands at the time, but I finally attached that button. I presented my work to the headmistress just minutes before she screamed for the kids to clean up after dinner. She grabbed the jacket from my hands, examined it, looked down her crooked nose at me, and frowned, or scowled really, like she was remindin' me this did nothing to erase my crime. I darted through the dining room door and climbed onto a chair at the table. That pea soup never tasted so good."

"Dang, I'll bet," I said with a laugh.

He paused a minute and pivoted the conversation. "Why don't I ask you a coupla questions?"

"About me?" I squeaked, still tapping out the last of his sewing story. I learned after my first phone call with Phantom that I needed to record our conversations if I ever wanted to get it all down, but I felt the need to type notes as backup.

"Yes, ma'am," he said bluntly but kindly.

"OK," I laughed uncomfortably. I don't know if this is typical of journalists or if it's just me, but I hate sitting on the other side of the questioning. I'll admit, it's a control thing. I prefer to steer the conversation.

"What do your parents think of you writing about an old mountaineer on the other end of the continent?"

He must have thought I still lived with my parents. My voice sounds like I could be in high school, which doesn't help. "Well, to be honest, it's my husband who's most concerned about how I'll find time to do it. But my mom is excited about it. We don't see each other that much, though. She lives in South Dakota, that's where I grew up. And my dad, well, he passed away a few years ago."

"Oh, I'm sorry to hear that, hon." I looked at my list of questions to return the spotlight on him, but he interrupted my thoughts with, "Well, what do you think he'd think about it?"

Now he was the one digging too deep, too early. I opened my mouth to respond but paused when I realized I didn't have a canned answer for this. Most people who stumble onto the fact that I lost my dad before I graduated college, before I'd met my husband, before I'd set out into my career, take the first U-turn the conversation allows. Phantom must feel like he's got the right to ask people almost anything because he's usually the one on the other end of the prying.

I swallowed hard before saying softly, "I think he'd be really excited about something like this." He didn't make a sound, so I offered a little more. "He'd like you and enjoy hearing about the life you've lived. He read almost everything I ever wrote. I think just to be supportive more than for the enjoyment of it. But yeah, he'd definitely be into this."

"Sounds like a good father," he said softly, as though he wanted me to continue.

"My mom has always supported my writing, too," I felt the need to add. "But Dad would go over the top with excitement. That's how he was with everything he did." Phantom let out a subtle laugh, maybe because he could relate. "Most weekends when I was in college, we'd catch up over the phone about school. We usually talked about the news, politics, and national stories mostly, and also whatever I was working on that week for the school paper. He'd offer his own story ideas. I pursued a couple of them, but most I found plenty of reasons not to."

I paused a second thinking he had heard enough, but he stayed silent long enough that sharing more seemed the only option. "One of the first weekends he and my mom came to visit me at school up at Minnesota State, I took them to a basketball game. That's the only sport our school was any good at. After the game, when we were walking out of the arena with the rest of the crowd, my dad spotted a newsstand with a pile of the college's newspapers, and my article happened to be front page. Before I'd noticed, he grabbed the paper in his hand and was waving it over his head. 'That's my daughter on the front page. Look at that! This is her,' he pointed right at me. I'm pretty sure my cheeks were as red as our school colors." I laughed, and Phantom joined me. "I rushed him out the door and to the car, out of sight. Man, I hated it at the time. But now I miss it I guess."

"Sounds like a real outgoing guy," he added.

Something about the voice on the other end of the line made me feel, for a half-second, that it was Dad I was talking to. I mumbled, "mmhmm," and offered an uncomfortable chuckle as I realized I'd let the interview take a major rabbit trail. "So, there you go. OK, back to you—"

At that, someone must've knocked on his door. "Just a minute, hon." A few seconds later he returned to the phone, "I have a neighbor, Carmen, who's trying to fatten me up. She's here with dinner, so I better call it a night."

We both snapped back to the present.

"Oh yes, sounds good. I'll catch ya next week."

"OK, hon. You have a swinging safari, all right now?"

I chuckled a little at his sign-off phrase. It made me feel like I might actually have an opportunity for some sort of adventure, even as I sat in my kitchen with a cup of dark roast in a quiet Virginia suburb. "Thanks, Sierra Phantom. You, too."

CHAPTER

Flutterbait

(n.) Bait that is cast and allowed to flutter down, resembling a dying fish.

NOT LONG AGO, Sierra Phantom tracked the days of the week by the traffic on Highway 395.

It runs all the way from Victorville, California, up through Carson City and Reno to bisect I-90 in Spokane, Washington, and then it keeps on through the Canadian border. But its stretch through the northern end of Inyo County certainly doesn't feel as though it could transport you to another country or connect you to the longest interstate in the United States. It's a narrow road that, for most of the week, is meant to carry the few locals from home to work to the grocery store and back. But one night a week, the road that cuts through the valley's darkest and most desolate desert terrain, shines as bright as the Las Vegas Strip, with thousands of headlights pointed north. For Phantom, that marked the start of the weekend.

For decades, the mountain man saw those headlights as a crowd waiting in line to ruin what he'd come to call home. But something was changing in him. He'd noticed, in the months since he moved into town, that his view toward tourists was starting to soften. He started picturing them just as folks who possessed that same sense of wonder that first drove him at twenty years old to abandon all he knew to hitchhike that same road north. Most of these people just wanted a taste of the life he'd gotten to live all these years, so he figured he ought to teach them how to preserve the place. Plus, he couldn't help but view that line of cars as pent-up demand for his new business.

By mid-summer, he'd become known as the local expert outdoorsman ready to guide anyone who had a few bucks and a few hours. His clientele ranged from elementary classes on their first high-elevation adventure to seasoned fishermen hoping the seasoned guide would reveal some of his secrets. He'd take the temperature of each group, see what kind of trip they were up for, and then usher them through all the High Sierra had to offer. They strolled down walking trails, waded through streams, leaped across boulders along the lakeshores, and navigated every inch of liquid in the area. He guided groups along trails from North Lake to Grass Lake that delivered them to grassy meadows busy with wildlife. With others, he charged up John Muir Trail where they'd run into backpackers with that virtuous glow that can only be drawn out by a weeks-long hike.

A lot of the tours went so well that customers invited their guide to end the day with them with s'mores over a campfire or hamburgers at a Bishop diner, giving Phantom permission to carry on about what wild berries to avoid or what tackle to live by until the tourists were too exhausted to hear anymore.

His customer base wasn't without its skeptics, though. One morning he took a group of retired guys who had driven from Oregon just to see if rumors of South Lake's ten-pound trout were true. Phantom talked all the way up the mountain about the best way to get one on a line. ". . . There are a half-dozen sporting goods stores in Bishop selling every kind of tackle imaginable, but my glitter flies guarantee a big catch. I'm tellin' ya, they can't resist," he said, his bony frame bouncing in their truck's jump seat with each turn toward the lake.

Phantom could tell by their silence they didn't believe a word he was saying. The overweight man in the driver's seat peered at the fishing guide in the rearview mirror, "So you use these glittery flies that look like something from a third-grader's art project to pull in ten-pound trout? And you're using a Zebco spincast reel?"

The big guy gave Phantom a bad time about the spincast reel—which he'd tossed in his truck bed alongside their overpriced whatevers twenty minutes earlier—because it's what beginners typically used. "Well, it's durable, which I need for all the backcountry fishing I'm doin', and the way it's designed with the spool fixed, it never gives me any trouble with backlash," he said in defense, before adding for good measure, "and my fishing record speaks for itself."

"I guess we'll see," the big guy mumbled, pausing a minute to turn off some old country song that was getting fuzzier as the truck climbed toward the lake. "So how'd you come up with these glitter flies?"

The question brought an eager grin to Phantom's face. "You know, it wasn't long after I moved up to the area. I was standing in this slow moving stream a few thousand feet above Bishop, casting over and over again like ya do. Being real patient. I watched the water closely as it set its course through the rocks, looking for my next catch. As I stood there, the morning sunlight shined so bright on that water like it was glitter. And right then I got this idea for a fly that shimmers. Awhile later I figured out how to keep 'em afloat. After shooting a deer, you knock off the hooves and boil 'em and scrape the film off the surface. That's the strongest epoxy anywhere. My flies carry so much oil, they can sit in water for years and they'll never sink. And I'll tell ya now, the first time I used one I caught seventy-six fish in the very lake we're headed to now."

"Oh, yeah—" the driver choked on the words, "seventy-six?"

"That's right. Ever since, I've been making and selling them, and I just keep hearing success story after success story."

"Well, I don't know," he stroked his scruffy chin and paused just long enough to make Phantom feel uncomfortable. Then, he added, "I think I'll just stick with my mini jig."

"Suit yourself." Phantom made sure to guide their boat as far away from his favorite spot on South Lake as he could. If he remembered right, they didn't catch much of anything that day.

ONE OF HIS FAVORITE TOURS that summer was with a Boy Scout troop from Fresno. The crewcut scouts lined up in a perfect row in front of Cottonwood Pass awaiting instructions. They wore the scout signature yellow neckerchief and stern faces to match, like the one Phantom carried through basic training.

"Wow, you guys really know how to put your best foot forward," he grinned. He gathered their troop leader was strict. Although, he was quick to leave them with Phantom for the morning. "Very impressive. The scouts are a great place to learn respect for nature, but let's have fun with it, too. Look at this place. We're in the middle of some of the most organic beauty this world has to offer."

He whipped his right arm up as if he were a circus ringmaster introducing the greatest show on earth. And, following his lead, the troop did a 360-degree turn to take in everything. Their heads tilted back to look up at the tops of the Lodgepole Pines, and almost as if he were cued, a red-tailed hawk circled above, eyeing the terrain for breakfast.

"Alrighty boys, you ready for an adventure?"

"Yes, sir," they said in unison as their heads snapped down to look back at their guide.

"Now, say it like you really mean it," he yelled. "Are you ready for an adventure?"

"Yesss sir!" they blasted.

"OK, now you've spooked all the wildlife," Phantom joked with a grin. A few laughed, and their shoulders seemed to relax some. "Why don't you take up the lead, son?" he pointed to one boy. "What's your name?"

"Devin."

"OK, Devin, start up the trail there, and everybody keep an eye out for wildlife."

After a while of working their way up the trail, climbing over fallen tree trunks, and ducking around house-sized boulders, their poker faces were replaced with wide eyes and grins. They charged up the trail, pointing out squirrels, berries, and wild flowers.

"Pretty great up here, huh?" Phantom asked at one point, his lungs working double-time to match their clip. "Now, tell me more about what you guys are learning in Boy Scouts."

One boy explained all the different merit badges they could earn, and another rattled off the scout's motto: always be prepared.

"That's a great motto to live by," Phantom added. "Living up here, I learned first-hand how important it is to be prepared for any danger."

They were really cooking up the trail now. Phantom stopped to catch his breath and get a drink of water. "Hold up, boys," he gulped in the dry mountain air. "Let's sit for a minute. Everyone bring water?"

They nodded and grabbed their water bottles before finding seats on a couple of boulders. "Our troop master said you lived in the outdoors like a wild man," one of the boys spoke up.

"Yeah, you could put it that way." He laughed and tilted his bottle of water to get a good drink. "You can't live like that without being prepared. Before I went into the mountains, I did all the research I could about what I was gettin' into. I knew I couldn't rely on good weather, easy hunting or fishing, or pure luck, because there isn't any of that up here. At that point, in the late '40s, the place was like a no man's land. There weren't even maps of the area or guidebooks and very little information about the weather patterns, so I found a couple of mountain guides who had worked up here. They told me I was nuts," he smiled and looked each of the boys in the eye. "Said that nobody could survive up here yearround because up until the early '80s, the storms were so severe. You're talking about eight to ten feet of snow, temperatures thirty, even forty below zero, and hundred-mile-hour winds."

That raised the boys' eyebrows. "But I'll tell ya, their warnings went in one ear and out the other. The wilderness was where I belonged."

"What about bears or mountain lions?" Devin asked. "You run into anything like that?"

"Oh yeah. At that time most figured there were about three hundred mountain lions along the range. But they never attacked people because they had enough to eat with all the bighorn sheep, the deer, and the smaller critters. So I had no fear of them. There were black bears, but they won't hurt you as long as you stay away from their cubs. Plus, animals have a keen sense of smell, and they know real quickly if you're a stranger in the woods by your scent. I became such a part of the wilderness out here, I began to smell more like them than the city before too long."

They sat silent, so Phantom kept going.

"I've never had a fear of animals. Ya know, some people just have a thing for working with them. Take these hummingbirds that come to a feeder outside my apartment. For the past month I've been admiring these birds. Tiny things, but so beautiful in chartreuse, yellow, blue. They'll fly two inches from my face and just buzz there for thirty seconds as if they're saying, "Thank you, Sierra Phantom, for that little feeder.'"

"My dad says I got that," a skinny blond-haired boy spoke for the first time. "A special way with animals."

"Oh yeah. You have pets?" "Yes, sir. Two dogs, three cats."

"No one wants to hear about your pets, Adam," Devin scolded, his feet dangling from the boulder above them.

"I'd like to hear about 'em," Phantom assured Adam. "Wow, you really have a full house with two dogs and three cats." He stood up, took another slug from his bottle, and motioned the boys to continue the hike. "Do you help with them?"

"Oh yeah, I take care of them on my own mostly," the boy said matching Phantom's pace. "I actually have two badges from working with animals: my pet badge," he paused a moment to point it out on his green sash, "and my animal science badge. You have to do more than just have pets to get the animal science badge."

"Oh yeah?"

"My mom works at an animal shelter, so I volunteer there in the summer. I clean their cages and fill food and water dishes, but most the time my mom just wants someone to play with the cats and the dogs and a pig. They just got a potbelly pig."

"Man, you sound like you know what you're—" "Shh!" one of the boys at the back commanded.

Phantom turned around to see the boy pointing toward a young doe standing less than a hundred yards away. Without a sound, they each dropped to their knees.

"Wow, she's a beauty," Phantom whispered. Her big ears, like satellite dishes, twitched slightly, surveying the area for danger. "Adam, you think you can go up to her without spooking her?"

"Huh?" the boy's eyes widened.

"Yeah, you'll do great. Take this." Phantom took a bag of peanuts out of his shirt pocket and filled the boy's little palm and then tapped his shoulder to encourage him along.

"OK . . ." his eyes grew even bigger, and he held his breath as he gingerly started toward her, the peanuts leading the way. Phantom held his index finger to his mouth to motion the boys to keep quiet.

"It's all right, girl," Adam looked straight into the doe's eyes, "no one's going to hurt you."

Within a few seconds he was three feet away from her. Phantom and the boys sat breathless with eyes fixed on the scene as if even a blink would spook one of them. Adam paused, probably feeling like his heart might thump out of his chest. The doe first nudged his hand and then licked his palm clean.

His grin might have been the thing to finally scare the doe away. She hotfooted it in the opposite direction and disappeared through the maze of trees. The boy stood motionless, his hand still outstretched. He finally dropped his arm and turned to look at his audience, his mouth hung open in the best kind of shock.

And the troop erupted with shouts and applauses. "Woa hoo!" "That was amazing!"

"Way to go, dude!"

"A true mountaineer," Phantom added, waving him over. "I'll report back to your troop leader that you have, by a long shot, earned your wildlife badge." Adam took one last look through the trees where the deer had exited and finally hiked back to the group, where he was met with a half dozen high fives.

Phantom delivered the boys back to the trailhead, where their troop leader, wearing a look as rigid as a retired Marine, sat on a boulder gulping black coffee. Each boy fought for airtime to tell him his version of the day. "We saw a deer . . ." Adam started.

"Adam fed it," another yelled. "It ate out of his hand."

"I'm sure their stories will keep you entertained all the way back to Fresno, sir," Phantom smiled, his cowboy hat in his hands. Without returning the grin, the man handed over sixty dollars and pointed to Phantom's Huffy. For most of the tours, Phantom asked the groups to drive him up the mountain, and then he coasted back into town on his own time.

"See ya, boys," Phantom yelled to the scouts, who were loading the van and digging for seatbelts.

Adam took a U-turn to run back to him. "Thanks, mister." He looked up at the mountaineer and stretched out his hand for a shake. Phantom bent down to give him a hug. "Great to meet you, bud. Keep lookin' after those animals, and come back when you want another adventure."

"Come on, boys," yelled the troop leader, who was now in the driver's seat.

"OK, see ya," Adam said one last time and ran to the van, which bolted out of the lot, kicking up gravel, as soon as the passenger door slammed shut.

HE COASTED BACK INTO TOWN that afternoon to spend the rest of the day in front of Schat's. He wanted to beat the rain he could tell was on its way. He grabbed a sandwich and a coffee from the gals inside and got to work on his flies, which he was working on every chance he got to keep up with the summer's demand.

Once he got settled on the patio, a couple of high school boys whom he often ran into glided along the sidewalk on their skateboards. He had met one of the boys, Derek, a few years back when he was still living up the mountain. A quiet guy who was also new to townie life. He grew up in a tiny mining village out in the middle of nowhere and finally moved to Bishop for high school. Phantom liked him.

He had a friend with him lately though who seemed put off by the old guy who loitered in front of the bakery. He was a messy-haired kid who seemed to always avoid making eye contact with Phantom.

"Hey, man," Derek mumbled in Phantom's direction while flipping up his skateboard with his feet to grab it with his hands in one fell swoop.

"Howdy, boys. How are ya?"

"Oh . . . pretty good. Pretty bored," he sighed and sat at the table next to Phantom. School was ready to start up again in a few weeks, so kids were running out of things to do.

"Bored? You guys are usually busy with some sort of outdoor adventure." Phantom was sure these boys were exactly how he would have been in high school, had he made it that far in school. It seemed they were always on their way to hike or rock climb or ski or some other exploit they hadn't yet decided on. On the nicest days, they couldn't resist cutting class to snowboard down Mammoth Mountain or climb through Rock Creek Canyon.

"Yeah, well, we don't want to get caught in this rain that's coming."

"Oh yeah, I hear ya there." Phantom dug in his shirt pocket for a business card and presented it to Derek. "You know where to come if you boys want a new adventure. If you get together fifty bucks, I'll take ya on the best fishing trip you've ever experienced."

"I know, I know," Derek said with a smile. "I already have your card."

"How 'bout you?" He directed the question toward Derek's friend, who hadn't stopped attempting some trick over the curb. "What's your name?"

"Travis," he said with a tough-guy nod, and he gave one more jump over the curb with his board, this one successful, before making his way toward them.

"You want a guided tour? Fishing or hiking? I bet there's some spots you don't even know exist just a short drive from where we're sittin' right now." He handed him the card Derek turned down.

He set it back on the table and took a seat next to them. "I don't think you want me to have that."

"Course I do. The more people know what sort of knowledge I got to pass on, the better." The kid didn't respond.

Phantom took off his cowboy hat, leaned forward to look him straight in his eyes, and said, "I know what I'm talking about, kid. I lived up in the High Sierra most my life. I learned firsthand how to survive, how to preserve nature, how to appreciate all we got around here. I experienced things no one else has." He leaned back in the metal chair and stroked his beard for effect.

"Oh, I don't doubt that, sir. But my father is Peter Young. You know, the fish and game warden up here."

"Oh yeah, I know Pete. We go back, him and me," he forced a smile and leaned back in his chair. Living out in the wild for years is the sort of thing game wardens will hunt you down for, but Phantom had no reason to run anymore. "I don't live in the wild anymore, kid. I've got a place of my own." He jerked his head south, "Just down the street."

"Listen," Travis said softly, "I know you know your stuff. I've heard people say they were sitting all day, catching nothing, and here comes this old fishing dude with his glitter flies, and they catch a huge one in one cast."

"Well, all right then," Phantom said with a satisfying nod. "There ya go." "Well, I hate to be the one to tell ya . . ." Travis hesitated half a second, looked down at his shoes and then back in the mountaineer's eyes. "You don't exactly have a permit to run a mountain guide business, and some don't like it. They see it as unfair competition. Word has got out about what you're doin'. I'm just sayin' be careful, that's all." "I'm not causing any trouble," he snapped.

The boy's eyes dropped again. Phantom put his cowboy hat in its place and started packing his flies in his briefcase. "You know, I figure they should be thanking me for teaching people about how to preserve nature and all the beauty up here."

"Hey, man, can I get ya a sandwich?" Derek asked, hoping to diffuse the situation.

"No, thank you," he said, trying but failing to soften his tone. "I'm callin' it a day."

The boys went inside to get lunch and left Phantom to his thoughts. "Who do all these guys think they are? If anyone should be kicked out of here, it's those people who commercialize the place, charging hundreds of dollars to let you float down Owens River or drop a line in Bishop Creek. Most of 'em don't even know what in the hell they're talking about anyway."

He snuffed out his cigarette on the bottom of his boots and started pedaling down Main. He kept his eyes on the sky with each rotation of the pedals. The fluffy, marshmallow-like clouds that started the day had come and gone, and heavy dark clouds had moved in. He heard a few drips on the brim of his hat, then a few more until it really started coming down. He picked up his speed . . . taking his usual left on East Lane Street, gave a nod to a couple of pedestrians waiting for the light to change, and then took his next right.

And then it happened.

He felt a massive shove from his left, like a four hundred-pound tackle ramming through him. It launched him high enough that he could see a ruby red minivan screeching to a stop below him. And he plummeted past it to kiss the black, wet asphalt of Sneden Street.

CHAPTER

Nibble

(v.) Getting a bite from a cautious fish but missing the catch.

HE WOKE TO THE SCREAM of an ambulance's siren, followed by the hurried shuffle of EMTs' shoes on the pavement. Two men gently tilted his body, while another slipped a board between him and the street. Seconds later, he heard ambulance doors slam shut and felt the prick of a needle in his right arm, and he blacked out. While the ambulance took his beat-up body to Northern Inyo Hospital, his mind transported him back to Alaska 1943, one of the most hated years of his life. Flashbacks from his years in the Navy still haunted him. They usually came at the darkest hours of the night, when deep sleep left him off guard.

This time it was as if he could feel the ground shake, and hear the rumble of bombs peppering the landscape behind him. He couldn't see them, but he knew that sound, like rolling thunder. It triggered his whole body to brace in fear. He turned, and finally something came into view: a dozen young men kneeling on the cold white surface, their olive green uniforms the only color for as far as he could see. He leaned toward them until their faces came into focus.

They looked up at him as if they were awaiting instructions. "God, they look desperate," he thought. "Scared, hungry, freezing. All they're wearing are those goddamn Navy-issued jackets as if they were fighting in California in the springtime."

"We've gotta find food," he barked, the words gobbled up by the groans of fighter planes overhead. "And for God's sake, make a shelter. Pile up this snow, and make an igloo. Make it as big as you can. We gotta all fit in there and get warm. Do you know what I mean?" He yelled so loud his lungs hurt, but the boys didn't react. He stopped to stare at them, begging for a response, until he figured they were too stunned to speak. So he kept on. "Coupla you boys come with me. We gotta get food if we're gonna make it through the night."

He turned away from the drone of battle and began to wade through the snow. It felt like tar beneath his boots. He lifted leg after leg through the awful stuff, his frustration growing with each weighty step. He finally looked over his shoulder to see he hadn't made it but a few feet. "Aren't you coming, boys?" he growled to the picket of soldiers. He leaned in to see if they had heard him over the planes. When one of the soldiers came into focus, he saw his ear had the undeniable burn of frostbite.

"Come on, you've got to get shelter!" he grabbed the boy's shoulder to shake a reaction out of him. He didn't move, like he was frozen in place.

Phantom leaned in closer to see that all of them were stiff, staring at him dead-on with no life left in them. His legs gave out in shock and landed him on his back. And he lay there, as if strapped down, staring at a colorless sky. He heard the whine of a fighter plane. His eyes searched the space above him until they spotted the thing barreling toward him. A big red circle glared at him from its side as if it were a hawk's eye scouring the ground for its prey. The Japanese. He tried to scream, but the sound was trapped in his lungs.

"You know him?" He heard a woman's voice from a distance.

"He's that guy who sits out in front of the bakery . . ." a man answered. "Come on, man. You're OK."

"Ahhhhghh," Phantom awoke with a real scream this time. "Ah . . . Ah . . . Where am I? What's going on?"

"Mr. Glover, you're OK. You've been hit by a car, but you'll be OK." And it all went black again.

WHEN HE REGAINED CONSCIOUSNESS it took him a minute to figure out where he was and what had happened. He opened his blue eyes to a room that was so bright it sent a shot of fiery pain behind his eyes and forced them shut again.

He must've taken a beating, he thought as his brain registered the rest of his body. All 120 pounds of him ached.

"Morning, Mr. Glover," he heard a bubbly nurse say. He lifted his eyelids just enough to see her move across the room to the window, where she pulled down the blinds. "How's that?"

"Much . . ." he cleared his throat. "Much better."

She came to the bedside and asked, "How are you feeling?" "Well, everything hurts. My head hurts the most."

"You really got rattled, but I think you'll do fine. The doctor will be in to talk with you in a few minutes. In the meantime, let me get you breakfast."

"No, no, I'm really not hungry." He worked his aching frame up the bed to sit straight. "A coffee and a cigarette will lift my spirits, though."

She gave a small laugh, "I wish I could. The doctor doesn't want you having caffeine, and there's no smoking in here. But I can get you a cup of decaf."

"Oh, all right. Thank you, hon."

When she left, Phantom made his way to the bathroom. He knew she'd probably escort him there if he didn't do it while she was gone. He did his business and then caught a glimpse of his beat-up face in the mirror. A red and purple bruise surrounded his right eye, and bloody scrapes from the asphalt stretched from his cheek to his forehead. He let out a sigh as he took it all in. "Damn," he thought. He looked like he'd aged ten years, and he felt it, too.

As he shuffled back to his bed, he heard, "You're looking better, Mr. Glover." A smiling man in a white lab coat stood in the doorway. He pulled a hard, plastic chair from the other side of the room to Phantom's bedside and sat down. "I'm Dr. Brown."

"Call me Sierra Phantom," he said slowly, feeling even lower on energy after seeing his state.

"You've greeted me on occasion around town." He paused a second to give his patient a chance to say he recognized him. Because Phantom didn't, he sat silently until the doctor waved his hand, "Oh, never mind. Don't expect you to remember. Seems like you greet about everyone you see."

"You do look familiar," he finally chimed in to be polite. "Nice to meet you, or, I guess see ya again, Doc."

"Here, I want you to drink this." The doctor handed him a can of strawberry Ensure. "The nurse said you didn't want breakfast, but you need to get some protein."

He conceded and pulled the tab open to take a sip. "So what's the verdict?"

"Well, I don't have to tell you, you really got slammed. Your head took the brunt of it—your face hit the pavement—and your eyes are going to need some serious work."

"Sounds about right for how I'm feeling."

"One important thing to know is that this incident was a hit and run," he continued in a calm, measured tone. "The police don't have a clue who it was. They don't even know if the driver saw you."

"Oh, she saw me," he interjected. "I remember her brakes screeching." "Well, they'll keep looking for her. They'll probably contact you to see if they can get a description. Odds are she was up here on vacation and won't be easy to find. But what this means is that we don't have her insurance to send all these medical bills to."

"So I'm hit by a car, and I'm paying for it, too. Is that what you're telling me?"

"We'll work with you on the payments, and I'll do my best to see what the hospital can take care of. But you need to know that going in."

This news, that somehow made every inch of him hurt worse, settled in while the doctor put him through countless tests to figure out what shape he was in. Dr. Brown blasted a puff of air at his pupils, flipped up his eyelids, and flashed lights at him until his eyes watered in pain.

After a few hours of looking over the tests, the doctor returned to the room to say he had a dose of bad news and a dose of good news. He said the accident really rattled his eyes, and he would need a special kind of surgery. "In hospital lingo, special means expensive," Phantom thought.

"You're going to have to undergo several operations," he said, flipping through a clipboard of documents. "You'll need a stent in your eye and an artificial tear duct to get everything flowing like it should."

All Phantom could manage was a sigh as he dropped his head in frustration. The doctor sat down next to his bed and softened his tone. "None of that is cheap; I know, but I have an idea. I made a couple of calls and got you an appointment at the Jules Stein Eye Institute at UCLA. Everything they do is state-of-the-art, and they're always looking for patients to test out new procedures for free. They're some of the best eye doctors I know. I told them your story, let them know you're really an important figure in this community, always helping people out."

Phantom lifted his head, "Really?"

"As long as you can get a ride down there over the next few weeks. You really shouldn't be driving."

"Oh, I don't have a car anyway. Never even had a license. I'll ask around for a ride." He smiled and offered as firm of a handshake as he could muster. "I'll get you some of the best trout on this earth as a thank you, soon as I can get my line back in the water."

"Sounds like a deal," Dr. Brown smiled. "Just rest up for now."

To keep himself busy that afternoon, the nurse brought him an article the local newspaper ran on his accident. Squinting to see the words only worsened the pain, so he asked the nurse to read it to him.

"Well sure," she said, lifting the paper to her eye level. "Let's see, 'Bishop Police are looking for a driver who hit a bicyclist Tuesday. The man is recovering at Northern Inyo Hospital with non-life threatening injuries . . .'"

He only got a few paragraphs on page six, but it got him thinking. He should get the newspaper to tell his whole story—share with Bishop who he really was and get some advertising for his business while he was at it.

He convinced the nurse to bring him a phone, and a minute later he had a reporter from the Inyo County Register on the line. "I think I have a story you want to hear," he said, hearing no response. So he kept on. "Yeah, so I lived up in the High Sierra most my life, and now I want to let folks know about my mountaineer and fishing guide business. I've had all these adventures, and I think people would want to hear it for themselves."

"Is this Sierra Phantom?" He just barely made out what the man on the other end of the line was saying over the police scanner and newsroom chatter.

"Well, yes."

"I've seen you around. We've actually talked a couple of times in front of the bakery."

"Oh, yeah? OK, well good. What do you say then?" "I'll hear what you have to say."

He was at Phantom's bedside the next morning. A guy that looked a week out of college. That's probably all they can get in this little town, so far away from any exciting headlines, Phantom thought. He was overdressed for Bishop, in khakis, a crisp button-up, and a tie like he was trying to make up for a lack of experience.

"Matthew." He extended a hand.

"Howdy, Matthew. Real name is J.P. Glover, but you can call me Sierra Phantom."

He took a seat in the plastic chair, flipped open a narrow notebook clutched in his left hand, and dug for a pen in his shirt pocket. He wrote something at the top of the page and finally looked up.

"So, you said you had a story for me?"

"Oh yeah, a front-page-kinda story," he flashed a promoting smile. "But first, will you please pass this on to someone in classifieds?" Phantom handed him a sheet of paper with a request for a ride down to LA.

"Sure," he looked down at it. "They charge by the word count, so they'll call you. You can just pay over the phone with a card or something." "Alrighty . . ." and then Phantom started where he always started.

In his early twenties looking for an escape. ". . . So I first hiked to Lake Isabella, which sits at a lower elevation of 2,500 feet. I spent three weeks studying how much vaporization was in the air, the type of fish it provided, and the different types of herbs and animals. That gave me a pretty good study. And as I hiked higher in elevation, I learned more and more about each spot."

The cub reporter scribbled in his notebook and every couple of seconds looked up at Phantom before returning to make another note. "I eventually made my way to South Lake to set up my first camp. It seemed like the best place to get started. There's a stream there that moves fast enough that it never freezes. There were a few edible plants nearby like manzanita bushes and sweet cicely—which is an herb—and blue camas bulbs, so I was set.

"Well, after a few months getting situated there, I started setting up more camps, each about fifteen to twenty miles apart. I'd hike up, study the area for a few weeks, and pick the best spots I could find. Eventually, I had eight camps that covered a hundred miles. I'd rotate through 'em—stay at one for a couple months, then leave it all just as I found it and move on to the next. There were a few reasons for this. I didn't want to mutilate an area—I wanted to respect all that the High Sierra offered— and I also didn't want rangers finding me. State law only allows people to camp in an area for two weeks . . ."

He paused long enough to give the kid time to get that last thought down. Some moments he'd scratch his blue pen over his reporter's notebook as fast as he could to get a sentence down before Phantom went on to the next, and then other times he looked up at him with an uninterested stare. But Phantom kept on.

"As soon as I had my camps in place, I felt I could relax a little and just enjoy all the beauty that surrounded me, and then I'd—"

"Didn't you miss being around people? Friends or family or just other human beings?" The kid emphasized the last words in a tone that Phantom found insulting. It bothered him that people always asked him that, as if human beings offered something more than Mother Nature.

"Hell, no," he snorted. "After the war and everything else, I didn't want anything to do with people anymore. If they wanted to go blow up the world, let 'em do it. Just leave me out of it."

The reporter scribbled wildly on his pad, flipping pages before they were filled. Phantom took a sip from the day's first can of Ensure while he tried to calm his nerves. He sighed and worked to rein in his tone, "I mean, I just considered Mother Nature my family. I just felt like I was finally home. Most people might feel intimidated living miles from people, surrounded by these elements that are so beautiful one moment and life-threatening the next. But not me. I loved every minute of it."

"Wait a minute," Matthew finished a thought on his pad and looked up. "What prompted you to abandon everything and live up there anyway? You said you fought in the war . . . World War II? Where were you stationed?"

"Alaska," he opted for the least threatening of the questions. "Few people know that a lot of the fighting against the Japs was done there. The Navy kept it pretty quiet at the time. But I gotta tell ya, I couldn't believe my luck when they told me where I'd be stationed. As a kid, I read books about the beauty of the Alaskan wilderness and the arctic wildlife . . ."

He took another gulp of Ensure. ". . . As soon as I stepped off the plane, those books came to life. All of it was so beautiful; I felt like Alice stepping into Wonderland. To this day, I can name the complete island chain. I actually thought I'd get back there to work as a fishing guide or something."

"So, what was the war like?" the reporter asked, looking at Phantom straight on as if he were asking for the weather forecast.

Phantom took a deep breath, sat up straight, and told him he wouldn't be going into all that. He gave up four years of his life to fight the Japanese, and he wasn't giving them another minute's thought if he could help it.

"I was just eager to get away from it; that's all," he said, slow and measured. "Let's just keep it to the mountaineer stuff. I just want to let people know I'm here, I'm experienced, and I want to share all I've learned. Alrighty?"

"Yes, sir," he nodded, and he shut his notebook with the same look a fisherman wears after a big trout slips away. "I'll get this in next week. I'll keep it at what you told me and make sure readers know where to go for a fishing guide."

"You got all you need already? Well, let me give you my business card," he dug his hand into his brief case beside the bed. "You can put all my contact information in the article."

The reporter exchanged his card for the mountaineer's and left.

Asking For Help

I'm looking for a ride to UCLA within the next couple of weeks so I can get surgery on my eyes.

Gas, other expenses will be covered. If you can help, call 760-555-0981.

Thank you!

J.P. Glover aka Sierra Phantom

CHAPTER

Dig

(v.) Technique used to unearth information
that sources want hidden.

"HELLO, PHANTOM HERE." Each week, I looked forward to those friendly words.

"Mr. Phantom, how are ya? Is now a good time to talk?"

"Well, hey there. Yeah, now's good. I'm just coming in from the grocery store. They had a sale on canned-everything—peas, carrots, beans, chili—so I'm stockin' my shelves." Then he launched into his dinner plans, "I got a frozen pizza, too, and I'm thinkin' I'll throw some chili on it, really make a meal out of it. I always try to enjoy every meal, even when I was out in the wild I wanted to really savor every bite of whatever I was having 'cause it was usually a lot of work to get."

I laughed a little at how quickly he could draw our conversations back to the preferred years of his life. "Just a second, hon," I heard the rustle of grocery bags and a refrigerator open and close. "OK, now let me tell ya how I got my food up there . . ."

"OK," I consented. Each time we talked, I tried to give him a few minutes to go on about whatever was on his mind before I guided our conversation back to my list of intrusive questions, like enjoying dessert first might help him choke down, say, canned peas.

This is Journalism Rule #2: ease into the hard-hitting questions. Make a source feel comfortable, like they're catching up with an old friend, and then, if all goes as planned, whatever question you're guiding them toward feels less unwelcome. It was his earliest memories, years before he had found a home among California's peaks, that I wanted to return to.

"Every couple of months I'd come down to Bishop to restock supplies and sort of reset myself. I'd sell flies to get some cash and then buy enough carbohydrates to fill two five gallon buckets. Most the time I'd walk 'em back up the mountain that same day, unless I sold enough flies to get a motel room for a coupla nights. That gave me a chance to clean up my clothes, do any needed repairs on equipment, tie and sell a few more flies. Then I'd grab my groceries and walk back up the hill."

"OK, got it. So, what kind of groceries?" I offered.

"Well, the main idea is to figure out which staples give you the highest amount of energy with the lowest amount of weight. Anything else, you don't take. So I'd buy oatmeal, powdered milk, spaghetti noodles, chili beans, sealed bags of tuna . . ." he listed several other items, while I poured myself a mug of coffee. "I'd precook the chili beans and dehydrate them; see you're droppin' weight that way, and I'd do the same with vegetables. And I always saved a little room for a few chocolate bars. Up there a little treat like that really lifts your spirits. Then for my protein, I'd either pull it out of a lake, trap, or hunt. The trick with hunting is figuring out a way to preserve all that meat that you can't eat right away. I found the best way was to dry it. I'd cut venison in thin slices and cook it on low heat over a fire until it was so dry I could snap it like jerky . . ."

A minute later he started on how he hadn't been able to fish for a while and how he probably wouldn't get back on the water for weeks because a woman in a minivan hit him on his bike. He said it was a hit and run and the police hadn't bothered to look for the culprit. "Now the doc doesn't want me doin' anything that might be mistaken for fun. Hmm," he snorted. "I hate bein' cooped up like this."

He toned down his fiery comments with, "The doc was nice enough, though. He got me scheduled for surgery at UCLA. Says some of the best eye surgeons in the world are there. I just need to find a ride down there. So that's the thing I'm workin' on now."

At that point I abandoned any hope of following the second decree of journalism. "Mr. Phantom," I took a deep breath and sighed before jerking the conversation toward the question I'd had on my mind for days. "So what happened next?"

"What's that?"

"You know," I nudged and tried again, "last time we talked you were telling me about the orphanage. Man, that's all I've thought about all week."

"Yeah . . ."

"Well, can you share more about what happened there?"

"Well now, hon. I don't really like talking about those years." The words slid out of him as though they were rehearsed. He'd revealed as much as he wanted to about his childhood in the previous phone call. Even giving up glimpses of those years, to him, felt like a compromise. The rest would dissolve into time, without a trace, just as he preferred to live his life.

I shook my head and bit my lip in frustration. I'd blown it. I should've waited. "That's the end of that," I thought, as my eyes honed in on the blinking cursor on my computer screen, relentlessly pestering me for direction, the next word, the next question.

I looked down at my list of questions scribbled on my notepad and got ready to skip a half-dozen of them to ask about his first hunting trip or his first night sleeping under the stars. But then he interrupted my thoughts.

"Danielle, they were fourteen years of pure hell." His words were slower and softer than all the others about groceries and fishing. I could hear him pulling in heavy breaths and releasing them slowly. I bit my lip again, this time to keep myself from saying anything. "There are a lot of my early memories I wouldn't mind givin' up. From the time I was three to sixteen years old, I lived in four different orphanages and three foster homes." He raised his voice slightly, adding, "Dogs aren't even bounced around that much these days. It was different then. Nobody cared anything for orphans."

I heard the now familiar click of a lighter before he gained momentum, "Every one of 'em had their own way of operating. Each time I moved to a new place I had to learn the ropes. Most, like Parkland Lutheran Children's Home—where I lived the longest—were understaffed and overrun with kids, so the headmasters expected the older orphans to help manage the youngsters. It gave a lot of these older kids a head trip and a ticket to take out their anger on any kid who crossed them."

My fingers stopped typing to let the recorder do the work while I did my best to stay silent.

"At Parkland, these kids were called honor students. Throughout the day, their job was to make checks. They looked at how the beds were made, how well the potatoes were peeled, how well your schoolwork was done, you know, things like that. If your bed wasn't made right, you got two demerits. If they found a dirty dish, another demerit, and it went like that. And we paid for those demerits every night. Once dinner was cleaned up, the honor students screamed for every one of the orphans to get to the basement. They pushed us through the doorway like little cattle and lined us up.

"'Glover!' one of the meanest boys would shout. He'd slap the end of the paddle to his palm as if he were a ball player warming up for a home run. 'Two for you.' I remember his eyes got real narrow as he came up with somethin' I did wrong. I swear most days they tallied undue punishments just for their sick enjoyment. 'Your bed was . . . lacking,' he sneered. I learned the hard way early on never to argue your case. It just multiplied the beatings. So, I turned around, touched my toes, and gritted my teeth. And I'll tell you, if the force didn't lift you two feet from the ground, he'd swat ya again."

Phantom paused to take in a deep breath and probably a pull from his cigarette. I stayed quiet as I thought about how to keep him going. Then I heard him say in almost a whisper, "This is the first time I've talked about this stuff. Those years were pure hell," he repeated the phrase again. "It just turns me sour thinking about 'em. The headmasters were in it for a paycheck from the government, and we orphans were treated like slaves."

The line went silent for several seconds until I realized he was waiting for me to move the moment along. Before I dialed his number that morning, I'd thought that after he got me talking about Dad, it was my turn to pry. But now I was the one who felt indebted.

No matter how many sources I've had to convince to share awful stuff, maybe from a soldier returning home with half his limbs or a father who lost his little girl to cancer, I've never known how to respond. I wish I could offer a "Oh yes, I understand," and launch into a version of my own awful. But I didn't have any of those. I never have.

"I don't know what to say, Phantom," was all I could muster. "Thank you for talking to me about this."

As if I hadn't said a thing, he cleared his throat and continued, "One night, after another round of beatings, I couldn't take it anymore. I was so ticked off. I had to get out of there. While the older boys shouted at one another upstairs for God-knows-what this time, I lay in bed with my eyes wide open cookin' up a plan to escape. It was winter in Washington, so I knew it wouldn't be easy. But I decided I'd go the next night."

As if he'd just realized how far beyond his gated past he'd let me discover, he stopped. I thought he was taking a moment to re-light or take a sip of something, but when I didn't hear anything more, I said, "Mr. Phantom?"

"Hon, why don't we take a break. I wanna get a few things done around here anyway."

While I hated leaving our talk on such a somber note, I wasn't about to object. "OK, thanks again. Hope you have a good day." That was a stupid thing to say, but I didn't know what else to say.

"Thanks, you have a swingin' safari yourself."

I forced a smile as if he could see me and hung up. I slammed my laptop shut and dropped my forehead to the kitchen table. I felt guilty. For making him relive those memories. But even more so, for nothing I did but for everything I couldn't do.

MY GROWING UP felt a world away from where our talks had taken us. As I said, I've never had much of a story of my own worth sharing; maybe that's why I'm drawn to everyone else's. I always considered my life pretty uninteresting, especially as a kid.

I was the middle child of a pastor and a teacher. My grandmother moved in with us shortly after I was born to serve as a loving surrogate parent when Mom and Dad were at work. Life was predictable. It was happy, healthy suburbia.

Looking back, I think my dad must've worked hard to make sure life for his children was exactly that because his childhood was anything but predictable. I didn't realize this until it was too late to thank him for it. He didn't talk much about his growing up. I suppose just enough to remind us to appreciate all we had. When he was teaching me to golf as a kid, he'd often say just before teeing off one of the prettier holes, "Man, we're blessed. You know that right?" I'd nod.

When he did offer glimpses of his childhood, his stories revolved around three things: his father, football, and his father's impossible expectations when it came to football.

MacMurchy boys pulled on pads and helmets by the time they were 8 years old. Through years of prodding from my grandfather, my dad earned the position of captain as a junior in a big Ohio high school. For what would be a coveted role for any teenage athlete, my dad never talked about it like that. His memories were branded with his alcoholic father's screams and occasional gut punches for fumbled balls and lost games. He told me that after one bad practice, he was forced to squat against the washing machine for hours until his legs could no longer hold him up. I'd heard that Dad even missed his grandfather's funeral because there was a high school football game to be played. And that disputes over cut or benched kids festered into crosstown rivalries among families who were once friends. "To him, football was king," I remember my dad saying of his father.

When he talked about it decades later, I could still hear in his voice the stress that he was under during years he should've been more worried about school work and girls. Like Phantom, my father had survival on his mind early on.

CHAPTER

Trolling

(v.) To fish by trailing bait behind a boat.

———

CHAIN-SMOKING AND PACING the parking lot is how Phantom spent the morning before his surgery. He hoped the two combined would calm his nerves until his ride arrived.

It wasn't the surgery that had him worried. It was the city. There were very few things that scared Sierra Phantom, but Los Angeles was one of them. It was a place where he couldn't control his own destiny, no matter how much preparation went into it. His survival depended on everyone else driving right, thinking right, acting right.

He'd spent the previous three days trying to find someone to drive him to LA, where he was scheduled to go under the knife of one of the best eye surgeons in the state. A Schat's regular overheard Phantom telling the bakery's owner he was worried he'd have to walk down there or miss the thing altogether.

"I've asked everyone I can think of for a ride. . ."

"I have a few days free," a woman's voice interjected. Phantom looked up to see the short gal who drove the blue pickup truck approaching the counter.

"Morning, ma'am." He worked to put a smile back on. "Now, wait a minute. Are you serious?"

"Oh sure. I'm not one to turn down an adventure. By the way, my name is Reynier. People just call me Rennie." She shifted her walking cane to her left hand and offered Phantom her right.

He ignored it and bent down to give her a hug instead. "Thank you, thank you!"

Shortly after noon the next day, he heard the rumble of that old Ford growling his direction down Clark Street. He put out his cigarette on the parking lot pavement and ran inside Apartment 14 to grab his backpack. He tried to calm himself with a couple of deep breaths while he fished for his keys in his jean pocket. He didn't want the ride down to be miserable for his generous chauffeur, so as he locked the apartment door, he attempted to grin as if he were headed some place fun.

"Howdy, hon," he yelled with a big over-the-head wave on his way to the truck.

"Morning," she said with a little wave out the driver's seat window. He laughed as he opened the creaky passenger door and hopped in.

"Mornin'? Hon, it's on to the afternoon now."

"Oh yes, it is, isn't it," she said with a bashful grin. "I'm not really a morning person."

"No shame in that," he lied.

While she navigated the Ford toward Highway 395, Phantom's hand started toward his shirt pocket for another cigarette. "Do you mind if I . . . ?" he asked, pointing to the pack.

"No, that's fine with me."

He cracked the window, lit the smoke, and took a few puffs before asking, "So, what part of Bishop you in?"

"You know that trailer park behind the bakery?" He nodded. "I live there with my son and my little dog, Becky. It's not much. Just a humble trailer. On the plus side, I can pick up a pastry from Schat's and be back in my living room before it even has a chance to cool."

"Hey, that's a deal," he smiled.

"You like that place you're in?" she asked.

"Oh, I don't know." He took a pull and released the smoke toward the crack in the window. "After livin' most my life in the fresh air it's tough to settle in to most any place."

Her eyes widened as if she had just woken up or just remembered what she'd wanted to ask him. "So you really lived like that?"

Phantom grinned, "Yeah I did, more than fifty years."

"I read that article about your guide business in the Register. It was great. I think people liked learning a little about the mysterious man who sits in front of Schat's," she laughed.

"Well, that reporter left out a lot of the good stuff, I'll tell ya that," he said, the words sounding sharper than he'd meant them to.

"Oh yeah?" Rennie nudged.

"I mean, he gave the basic bird's-eye view. But he didn't paint much of a picture about all I've seen and done," he bragged.

"Well, I thought he made you sound pretty tough," she shrugged. "He didn't even mention one of the most wild things that happened up there. When this killer storm tore through the area in '82." He glanced her direction. She looked content to listen to one of his most repeated stories, so he continued, "So all these flatlanders were up there for a long spring weekend in the mountains. Ya know, hiking up trails in their flip-flops and T-shirts, completely unprepared.

"Well, this snowstorm comes, and all these people, hundreds of 'em, get stranded up there. The rangers put the whole mountain under a kind of martial law because they were so overwhelmed. And because I know every nook and cranny of the High Sierra, I ended up hiking right to the worst of the storm to lead people out. I found families and Boy Scouts and all sorts of people suffering from hypothermia, hyperventilation, bumps, and bruises. It was a mess. I saved almost seventy people by the end of it. And I got pretty beat up, too. Got hypothermia, and both my hands and feet were frost bit. But I wanted to do it, ya know, to save these people's lives."

"Wow, that sounds pretty scary."

He held his pace, "I knew the storm was coming, too. I've always been pretty good at predicting weather patterns, and the more time I spent up there, the better I got. My mind became so clear I wasn't even guessing at that point. I just knew. I predicted the 1988 drought, and I knew decades ago that this whole place would warm up—and, well, here we are."

Rennie smiled and hit the "off" button on the radio, probably realizing neither of them would have any boredom to ward off, even on the most desolate bit of highway this side of the Rockies. Once they left Bishop behind, it looked as though the road just might be able to carry travelers to the other side of the globe if they had the time for it. The only visual interruptions were the mile-markers, which Phantom always liked to pay close attention to—tracking how far they'd gone and how far they still had to go—to keep his mind busy.

As the Ford hit its stride, Phantom really got going, launching into a new story every tenth mile-marker or so. He went on and on, while Rennie smiled and listened. He let her know about his years working as a carpenter in Seattle's China Town, about learning Chinese, about working in a traveling carnival for a summer, about his years teaching ice-skating lessons, and about being the first to introduce the corn dog to the Pacific Northwest.

"No way, really?" Rennie laughed in disbelief.

"Yes, ma'am," he looked toward her with a wide grin. "OK, that last one was a fib."

"Hey, I'd believe you. Seems like you're creative enough to come up with something like that."

About the time they passed the fiery-orange wildflowers of Lancaster, his stories tapered off. He lit another cigarette and asked Rennie, "So, are you a Bishop local?"

"No. . ." She looked as if she were admitting to a crime. "You'd call me a flatlander." The term Bishop people use for folks from Southern California.

He felt the need to say, "Well, that's OK."

"Before I retired, I taught special education and cleaned houses in Pasadena. Single mom—makes for a busy life," she sighed as though she was still tired. "Now I'm just enjoying spending my time however I want to. For the first time in my life, I can sit and enjoy a TV show. I watch some silly ones too, like 'Murder She Wrote' and 'All My Children.'"

"I've been watching some shows myself," Phantom added. TV was still new to him, so he liked to talk about what everyone was watching.

"Oh yeah? Like what?"

"You ever seen 'Hannah Montana?'" he grinned and nudged her arm with the back of his hand.

"What? That little teenybopper show?" she squealed. "No . . ." She smacked the steering wheel and laughed, "You really watch that?"

"I don't miss an episode," he said bluntly, trying to straighten his grin. Rennie laughed and held her hand over her mouth to keep herself from snorting. "Well, I'm glad they have one viewer who will balance out their demographics."

As the two caught their breath, Phantom unzipped his backpack and pulled out a white paper bag, which every Bishopite recognizes as a sack full of Schat's goodies. The two munched and talked until the desolate view out the truck windows turned to foothills and then cookie-cutter suburbs. Before long, it was a spaghetti bowl of freeways swooping beneath the heavy city air, which was enough for Phantom to consider doing a U-turn to head right back to the Sierra's blue skies. But Rennie had the wheel, so she delivered them to the motel just as the sun set.

AS HE HAULED THEIR BAGS up the stairs to their adjoining rooms, Rennie suggested they get dinner before bed. "Might be fun to try something we don't have in Bishop," she almost sang the words as she made her way up the stairs of the motel. "Maybe Chinese or some good seafood. Mmm . . . You like seafood?"

Phantom waited until they were in the room before he let her know he was not about to roam around Los Angeles past dark. "Sorry, toots, I'm not venturing out there."

"Well, I'm not saying we'll go very far," she continued, now digging through her purse for something. She pulled out a stick of ChapStick and quickly ran it over her lips before adding, "Maybe just down the street, see what kind of restaurants they have nearby. It's a safe neighborhood; I think you'll—"

"No, ma'am," he announced sternly. "Getting shot at in this godforsaken city is not the kind of adventure I'm up for. All ya hear on the news about this place is people gettin' murdered and run over and robbed. What the hell do I want to go be a part of any of that for?" He set his hat on the bedside table to show that he was settled in for the night.

Rennie, spooked, dropped the ChapStick to the floor. She picked it up and managed a smile. "Sure, no problem. How about ordering a pizza?"

"Now that sounds like a deal." He smiled, "I'll treat."

The pizza guy came and went, and Phantom made sure to take a couple of looks out the window up and down Hilgard Avenue before relaxing. The two stayed quiet long enough to let Phantom's fit over dinner dissipate.

After Rennie got settled on the couch with a slice of pepperoni and a Diet Pepsi, she picked the conversation up again. She started slowly with a forgiving grin, "So, you're not a big fan of the city?"

"No ma'am."

"But living out in the middle of nowhere never scared you?"

"No, not really. I felt more comfortable up there than any other place in my life. In the wild, you can plan for most any danger that might come your direction. I studied the area long enough that I felt prepared on every front."

"Sounds like you were pretty brave. I could never do something like that."

"Hey, you lived down here all those years. That's brave," he offered. They got quiet just long enough to notice the motel radio had been left on, playing a muddled Johnny Cash's "Ring of Fire." "There was one time I was scared."

He stopped and dug in his shirt pocket for cigarettes. "This OK?" She nodded. He took a long pull while she sipped her soda.

"In the wild, there were a lot of days where I had to get things done just to survive, like hunt, fish, repair my shelters. Then there were days off, sorta like weekends in the real world, where I would just enjoy all the High Sierra had to offer. One morning in the middle of summer, I decided to reward myself with a couple of those days off, so I got up and set out to track this stream from Whitney Portal to Lone Pine. You know, if you're following a stream, you're never in danger because you can just follow it back to where you started."

"Ooh, I feel like you're hinting at something here," she smiled.

He nodded and gave it away, "I'll tell ya now, I managed to find danger. I was busy luring in this beautiful trout when the river rocks beneath my hiking boots began to shake. My eyes shot up toward the top of the mountain. It took a second for my legs to react to what my eyes were seeing. A cloud of white powder was powering down the mountain toward me."

Rennie turned down the radio, which was now spouting off about discounted car repair.

"I ran down the mountain as fast as I could until my foot caught a rock, sending me tumbling down a forty-degree slope. I was flying toward a huge drop off, so I grabbed the first thing I could—a manzanita bush. I held on to that thing for dear life and prayed the avalanche wouldn't bury me. My life coming to an end at 21 after just a few months in the wild was not what I had planned. I closed my eyes and braced for the blow. This huge wave of energy blasted past me. Felt like a squad of linebackers were racin' over me. And after what felt like five minutes, I was happy to discover it didn't take me with it."

"Yikes," Rennie added with wide eyes.

"Well, my trouble had just begun," he interjected. "Before my relief set in, I looked around and realized I was trapped, and all I had on me was my cigarettes, a lighter and my hunting knife. The avalanche took my pack with it."

"No food or water," Rennie asked.

"It was all in the pack. I taught this in World War II, if it's a matter of you or your equipment, let the equipment go no matter what. You can replace your equipment but you can't replace your life," he said, repeating a line he often rattled off while leading tours. "I had about $1,500 in cash in there, plus food supplies, tent, sleeping bag and, of course, water.

"I'll tell ya, Rennie, I felt completely defeated. But I didn't have a second to sit and commiserate. I had to steady my feet on this sharp incline that was covered with this shale. This stuff was so fine it felt like any step would cause all of it to break lose and create its own kind of avalanche. So I took my hunting knife and dug down deep until I hit solid ground and placed my foot there and took a minute to assess the situation.

"In one direction was a big drop. If I would've fallen 50 feet further, I would've gone over. And in the other direction was a granite wall, about 30 to 40 feet high. There was no way of getting around that. I climbed my way to it and studied it closely—to this day, I don't know how a spider could get up that thing. You need cracks and crevices to climb a face that steep, and I couldn't see any way to do it. So I kept stalling it off, stalling it off. I sat there all night, dozing in and out of sleep, thinking over my options.

"I remember the sunrise waking me up the next morning to my situation. Now I was gettin' worried. I was so thirsty; all I could think about was water. I knew I had to make a decision. Finally, under a full moon that second night, I thought to myself, 'Hey man, you're dead anyway. You've got to at least try something.'

"I took off my mountain boots, tied them around my neck, and started up this cliff. It was nearly impossible. Took every bit of my strength and concentration. It was like my brain cut off any feelings of pain, and instead honed in on using every part of my body to scrape and claw my way up this damn wall. I lost four fingernails and two toenails, my pants were shredded, my shins and hands were bloody. But I made it to the top. I just laid on the dirt and caught my breath for several minutes, until I finally made myself stand up and start walkin'. I walked nine miles to the little town of Lone Pine. Exhausted, I stumbled into a little restaurant—I'm sure I was quite the sight—and I asked the gal behind the counter to whip up some milkshakes for me, 'cause I was so dehydrated. I'll tell ya one thing, nothing has ever tasted so good as those milkshakes."

"Oh my word, I can imagine," Rennie finally responded, as though she were returning from the danger of that slick cliff to the Motel 6.

"I asked the gal there to call the sheriff. When he came I told him I had no money but I needed a place to stay for a couple nights. So he set me up while I waited for my partner in San Francisco to send me $1,500 through Western Union so I could pay the sheriff back and resupply. As soon as I resupplied, I went right back into the mountains.

"I can't believe that wasn't enough to send you back home," Rennie added almost in a whisper.

That word home caught Phantom off guard. He wasn't sure what she thought home was for him, but he wasn't in the mood to go into it.

"Hell no," he said, trying to sound tough. "I'll tell ya the truth, giving up is the last thing that ever comes to my mind. I've been in enough situations in life that I've learned how to push through obstacles. As soon as most people run into an obstacle, they get spastic. Their minds go haywire, and that's because all the pressure they're under living in the city. Most of them don't think right because they're used to computers thinking for them.

"I'll tell ya, though, the avalanche taught me a lesson: don't ever rely on pure luck. That was the worst situation I ever had in the mountains. From then on I thought of, and prepared for, every possible thing that could go wrong. It became my mindset, and helped me survive more than fifty years up there."

"Mr. Phantom . . ." Rennie said, almost in a whisper.

"Yes, hon? And you don't have to use the word mister with me."

"It's almost one in the morning. We need to be at the doctor's office by eight."

"Oh, OK. You gettin' tired?"

"A little," she lied. She was exhausted.

"Well, let's call it a night then," Phantom stood up straight and smiled. He swung his backpack over his shoulder and started through the door that connected their two rooms, but before leaving, he felt the need to apologize for going on. "Ya know, once I get going about all these experiences, I just get caught up in 'em. Anyway, sleep tight." She offered a sleepy smile, and as he closed the door, he heard her whisper to herself, "So do I."

CHAPTER

Acclimate

(v.) The adaptation of an organism to environmental changes.

TO LOOK AT HIM, you wouldn't have thought the surgery was a success. Powder white bandages crisscrossed over the top half of a puffy, black and blue face. Every couple of hours, as the pain meds dissipated, he felt as if something must have gone seriously wrong, like he'd been pitted against a professional boxer and lost. Then a good dose of oxycodone would bring him back to a state of pleasantness and gratefulness.

Over a bowl of green Jell-O, he went on to Rennie about how fortunate he was to be in the care of "some of the best damn doctors in this country," and then how lucky he was to have met her, his "generous chauffeur." Before he would leave for home, he insisted on making the rounds to the nurses' stations and the doctors' offices to thank them and hand them his business card.

"You're ever up my way, give me a call. I'll show you some of the best Mother Nature has to offer—free of charge," he told them.

The four-hour drive home was mostly quiet. Phantom dozed off around Palmdale and slept until the Ford rolled past Big Pine, with only the occasional moan from the pain. Rennie kept the radio tuned to country, and hummed quietly along to Willie Nelson and later Patsy Cline, as if she were singing her traveling partner a lullaby.

AS THE WEATHER WARMED and his strength returned, Phantom started having his morning smokes in the apartment parking lot, just to take in those first few moments of fresh sunlight. He easily beat the rest of Bishop out of bed, so the only sounds were the birds chirping, squirrels playing the day's first game of tag, and his boots gently clicking against the pavement.

Each morning, during his slow, aimless stroll, his eyes couldn't help but settle on White Mountain Peak. Phantom always talked about it as if it were a woman, just as fighter pilots did their planes in WWII or men do their boats today. "She's the third highest peak in the state, after Mt. Whitney and Mt. Williamson," he would say. The point of her jagged crest touches the sky at 14,250 feet above sea level. She had always been his compass.

For months, catching a glimpse of her from town had been just a tease of his old way of living. But on a morning a few weeks after his surgery, as he mindlessly sent up puffs of smoke, he came to realize that she'd become a source of comfort, even from a distance. She was always reminding him that the place he called home wasn't going anywhere.

It was a symbol of warmth during what had otherwise been depressing days around the Valley Apartments. He got acquainted with the place, and how dreary it could feel, while he was doing his best to follow the doctor's orders to stay home. There were twenty people living on less than half an acre, yet it somehow felt lonely. Most of his neighbors stayed tucked in their little dens, with their blinds shut and TVs on. Some of them were just old and didn't have the energy to get out every day. But others didn't have much reason to do so. No family. No friends. No longer a draw to the wild beauty that surrounded their little town.

"It's time to cheer this place up." The thought came to Phantom like a spark in the woods, and his lips stretched into a smile. Giving his cigarette a final couple of pulls, he started dreaming up how he might turn Apartment 14 into his own habitat of sorts.

He snuffed out his smoke, wheeled the Huffy out of the apartment, and peddled toward Main Street. He arrived at the hardware store just as the clerk flipped a sign in the window to read "Come in. We're Open." He bought a bucket of green paint from a clearance shelf lined with colors that families had likely sampled and promptly returned. He chiseled open the paint can and immediately realized why he'd gotten such a good deal on it. It wasn't a sage green paint like grandparents might use in their kitchen; it was a green as loud and obnoxious as Phantom's brightest glitter flies. It practically glowed.

"It's perfect," he thought to himself, and he spent the rest of the morning coating every inch of the apartment with it.

The next day, he got to work on filling up the walls, scouring every thrift store in town for anything he might be able to make his own. The project only encouraged his usual hunt for bargains. Phantom had become a regular at all three thrift stores in town, and his first stop was always Hospice Thrift Shop, just a block away from the apartment.

"Morning, Maggie," he hollered as the bell above the door dinged on a Monday morning. She was one of about a dozen senior volunteers who kept the place going.

"Good morning, Mr. Phantom," she said, looking up from a pile of clothes. "Just looking today? Or you got something special in mind?"

That's the same line she delivered each Monday. He wasn't exactly a thrift store browser. He would describe himself as a strategic shopper. The store took in most of its donations on Saturdays and Sundays, so Phantom was at the front door by noon on Monday—giving the volunteers just enough time to set everything out but beating anyone else who wanted to take a peek.

His first stop was always the racks of men's clothes. They were tucked toward the back because most men don't think to visit a thrift store for clothes. Then he'd make his way to the home goods section, which was really just three dusty shelves crowded with tired clocks and blenders and countless other appliances people abandoned to make room for newer versions. But, Phantom thought it was worth looking. He swore he could always find something that he could do something with. For example, just a few weeks after he moved into Apartment 14, he found a coffee table that almost anyone else would've considered firewood. A small repair and a fresh coat of paint later, he turned it into his workbench.

"I've got my eyes open for anything I can hang on a wall," he told Maggie on this particular morning. "I'm giving my apartment a bit of a face-lift."

"You know, we had a gal bring in a stack of paintings over the weekend. I just put them out," she said, gesturing toward the back of the store. He didn't normally pay much attention to the stacks of old paintings and photographs in the back. Never seemed like there was much turnover on those shelves. But, to his surprise, Maggie directed him to five beautiful framed paintings. He couldn't believe anyone would give these away. Each of them fit the look Phantom was going for. One was an up-close watercolor of a bald eagle, and the others were mountain scenes. He swore one of them was of South Lake. He wheeled the stack of paintings home on his bike seat and spent the next day adding a bit more color to each of them. He lined up his glitter glue and put dabs of green on the trees, blue on the water, orange and pink on the wild flowers, just to make it all really shine.

To display his glitter flies, Phantom glued a thick strip of foam to four pieces of plywood that Erick was throwing out. He spent an entire night lining each of the boards with more than three hundred of his homemade flies before nailing them to the wall.

When it was all said and done, he stood in the middle of his living room with a smoke in one hand and a cup of coffee in the other to look everything over. "Whoowie . . ." he said with a whistle, his eyes scanning the lime-colored walls crowded with paintings of mountainous scenes and flies, their glitter glistening under the apartment's cheap fluorescent light. "Damn . . ." he took a pull on his cigarette in satisfaction, "I oughta charge admission to this place."

Most wouldn't consider Apartment 14 homey. It came off more as a makeshift shop peddling paintings and fishing tackle. Nothing about the place looked moved in to. No bed or dining room table. Instead, a couch piled with blankets sat behind the refurbished coffee table that served as a workbench just as often as it did a kitchen table. This was as settled in as Sierra Phantom would ever get.

CHAPTER

Chumming

(v.) A fishing technique by which bait or scent is released into the water to attract fish to take a lure or baited hook.

I KNEW IT WAS 4:00 A.M. in Bishop, but I started dialing anyway. Phantom mentioned at one point that I could call any time after 6:00 in the evening—because that's when he usually came in for the day—and as late at night or as early in the morning as I'd like.

"I only sleep a few hours a night," he'd told me. "While you people are sleeping, I'm creatin'. My apartment is more or less like a factory. I'm making my flies or painting pictures or refurbishing somethin'. So you can pretty much call any time a night. If I'm here, I'll answer. Otherwise, I'm out fishin' or selling my flies."

His diatribe ran through my mind on a Thursday morning before work as I weighed whether or not to dial his number. We hadn't talked for a few weeks. I felt the need to put some time between our last conversation, not knowing whether he was upset about my pushing him to share more than he wanted about the orphanage.

But I woke on this particular morning feeling like we needed to talk. I must've dreamed about his story the night before because when my alarm rang, I couldn't shake the image of a dirty-blond kid staring up at the ceiling from his narrow bed, like a prisoner coming up with an escape plan. I awoke feeling frustrated that I couldn't free him or comfort him or help him. I skipped my morning jog and instead made myself a pot of dark roast and called Phantom.

Sure enough, he answered with his usual bubbly, "Hello, Sierra Phantom here."

"Mr. Phantom, you're awake?"

He offered one of his deep-chested laughs, "Oh yes, hon. What'd I tell ya? I don't need much sleep."

I sighed in subtle relief. He sounded as he always did, as though he'd completely forgotten, or maybe forgiven, where my questioning had led us weeks before. "How've you been?" I asked. "You feeling any better?"

I poured my coffee while he talked about recovering from surgery and how he met "a real nice gal" who drove him down to UCLA. He figured he could return to his guide business by next week. "Now, I'm not exactly runnin' this by my doc, but I feel strong enough to get back out there," he said before redirecting his chatter. "So, should we get back to it? Where'd we end up?"

"Last time we talked?" "Yes, ma'am."

"Um, well . . ." I hesitated to make him go back there, but he sounded willing. "I think you were coming up with a plan to run from the orphanage."

"Oh, yes. OK, let me think now . . ." And in the same breath he started where he'd left off, "So at that point I was about 9 years old and tryin' to get the hell outta Parkland Lutheran Children's Home, up in Washington. I knew I had to come up with somethin' clever because the older kids were always trying to run, and they always got caught. If I was gonna do this, I couldn't get caught. It'd be better to not try it at all."

He paused. I heard the click of his lighter as I took a quick sip of my coffee and started typing.

"Well, every Friday evening, the orphans were corralled into the auditorium for a double-feature movie. They counted all of us before and after the movie. I knew if I could slip out shortly after the first feature started, I would have a two or three-hour window before anyone noticed I was gone. I remember the auditorium was real noisy on this particular night, which meant the teachers had plenty to distract 'em. I waited for the screen to go dark, and then I crawled to the back door. I sat there quietly for ten to fifteen minutes, waiting for a loud point in the movie. Then I opened the door and tiptoed out. As soon as I let the heavy door click behind me, I let out a sigh of relief like I had been holdin' it in all day.

"I remember standing there a minute to take in the night sky, bright with stars. Breathing in the cool air, I let my mouth stretch into a smile without anyone there to stop me. I already felt free. I stepped down the cement steps and glanced over my shoulder at the rows of run-down dormitories. As I gave the place one last look, I could almost taste disgust on my tongue, if you can taste such a thing.

"I finally turned around, picked up my pace, and ran across the property line. The moon lit my way as I slowed to a walk to catch my breath. I hunched as low as I could and marched through a field of frozen grass. I can still remember the crunching sound beneath my feet. Within minutes, I reached a dock at the lake where a bunch of private boats owned by some well-to-do folks bobbed up and down.

"Parts of the lake were already covered with a thin layer of ice, but I knew rowin' a boat to the other side of it was my only chance at a clean getaway. By land, there were only two ways to get off the island: the Lake Washington Floating Bridge or the Kirkland Bridge, and both had gatekeepers who were impossible to sneak past. The farthest point on the other side of the lake was about six miles, so I figured I could pull the boat on shore there and buy some time to cook up a more permanent plan.

"I remember jumpin' in the first rowboat tied to the dock and my feet slippin' on ice that caked the bottom, but I caught my balance and grabbed each end of the oars. I dug the paddles into the water, leaned forward, and pulled back as hard as I could. As the boat picked up momentum, I thought, 'Whew, you're almost scot-free.'"

I heard him stop to catch his breath or maybe get a taste of nicotine. He exhaled, "I felt good, leaning forward, digging the paddles in, and pulling back with my whole body, and doing it again, faster and faster. After several more strokes though, it felt like the boat was getting heavier." His words quickened, "Almost like it was fighting against something. Then I realized, goddamn it, the boat was sinking! The ice inside the boat must've hid a leak. It was a breach in my only shot at escaping.

"I looked up toward the shore I had just come from, already a couple miles away. I turned my head and squinted toward the other direction.

That shore—freedom—looked at least two miles out still. I thought fast, 'Am I going back to that godforsaken place, with nothin' but chores and beatings and pure cruelty?' I knew if I went back, I'd get the hell beaten out of me anyway for even tryin' to run. A flashback of that place was enough to scare me over the edge and into the ice cold water."

My fingers punched the keyboard keys as though they were trying to keep pace with the heartbeat of that little boy. I kept myself from saying anything, except for encouraging mumbles to keep him talking.

"Six months earlier, I was swimming in that same lake, having the time of my life," he sighed and laughed a little. "I was winning ribbons at the orphanage's annual May Day competition. I won every one of the swimming races that day, even got my name in the paper. Now, here I was in the same water, but this time I had no audience. No interview or photographs would follow. I wasn't swimming for a ribbon or a bit of recognition. This was for my freedom, for my life, ya know?"

"Yeah . . ." I answered without meaning to.

"Now the water had a thin layer of ice on top, so it felt like tiny pins were coming at me at all sides. I didn't wade or take time to think through what I was doing. I knew if I didn't move quickly, I'd freeze or drown. My arms flew over my head, and my stiff legs kicked, pulling me a few feet with each rotation. I saw a faint light on the opposite shore. With every stroke, I kept an eye on the glow.

"The slushy water pressed against my chest, and it got tougher and tougher to suck in each breath. With every stroke, my arms felt heavier, and my legs seemed to stiffen and slow. Looking toward the light, it looked so far still. It seemed impossible. I felt defeated and scared. I remember almost cryin' in exhaustion. 'This is it,' I thought. 'I can't do it.' My arms fell limp; I closed my eyes and began to sink."

My chin dropped, but I stopped myself from speaking.

"Then I got this surge of emotion, of anger and power, and that gave me the jolt I needed. It revived me back into action. 'I've got to make it; otherwise all those damn people back there win,' I thought. I kicked harder and pushed my arms through the water over and over again. 'The light was getting closer,' I told myself. I kept on for what felt like the longest five minutes of my life. Finally, my toes touched the lake's bottom, and the little strength left in my legs pulled me onto the shore. And I dropped onto the rocky beach, suckin' in the cold air."

"You must've been exhausted," I blurted.

"Oh man, let me tell ya. I was." He paused to catch his breath. "All I wanted to do was rest, but I couldn't. I was sure the temperature couldn't be much more than thirty degrees. I was shivering like hell. I knew I needed to warm up fast. There was a tree belt along the water, so I went in there to look for some dry wood to get a fire going. One of the older boys at the orphanage had shown me how to do it. I found a soft piece of driftwood and then a harder stick. Just like he showed me, I rubbed the stick on the driftwood as fast and hard as I could until the dust started to smolder. Then you gotta gently blow until you have a flame you can transfer to the kindling. It took me a while, but I eventually got the fire really going. I don't really remember dwelling on the risks I had taken that night, just falling asleep as quickly as I could get dry.

"I woke up early the next morning, hungry and cold. Although, thinking about the headmaster and the honor students waking up to find me missing warmed me a bit," he laughed, so I joined him.

I looked down at my watch to see that I had a few more minutes left before I had to leave for work. "So, here you are, just a little kid. And you're out on your own?"

"Yeah, well, that's when I started robbin' houses." I could almost hear his grin through the phone.

"What?" I gulped down the last of my coffee. "You're serious?"

"Yes, ma'am. I made my way to the Rainier Beach neighborhoods, just outside Seattle. I walked up and down a couple of quiet streets, thinking of the best way to cop some food and warm clothes. No one locked their houses in those days, so I figured if I knocked on the front door and no one answered, it was safe to go in. I can still remember my very first robbery. It was a house on a cul-de-sac with high shrubbery and no close neighbors." He paused a moment and then said, "That's the perfect target, ya know," offering this advice to me as if I were taking notes for my own burglary.

"I knocked three times and waited, pressing my ear against the door. Silence. I turned the doorknob and stepped in. It looked like a home with kids; they had nice furniture and a wooden train set in the living room. I hotfooted it to the kitchen, grabbed a paper bag, and stuffed it with as much food as I could carry. Then I ran upstairs to one of the kid's rooms. I pulled a wool jacket and snow boots from the closet. The boots were just a little snug on my feet, but they were better than sneakers that time of year. While I was trying on all this stuff, I heard the squeak of car brakes in the driveway, and before I could react, someone wearing heavy boots stepped through the front door."

"No way, really?" I whispered.

"Oh, yes," he chuckled, loving that his story had me hooked. "Whoever it was coughed, clearing the cool air from his lungs. He sounded like a burly man, no one I wanted to wait around for. I knew I couldn't make it downstairs in time, so I raced to the bedroom window and pushed it open. I crawled onto the roof, peeked over the edge, eyed the softest looking area in the grass, and jumped off. The landing went better than I expected, actually. Half the food dumped out of the bag, but it wasn't worth scooping it up. So I leapt to my feet and ran as fast as I could through a string of backyards.

"From that point on, I came up with a foolproof plan. Looking back now, I had a pretty smart mind for a kid. If there were no lights on in the house, that was pretty much a guarantee no one was there. But, to be sure, I knocked on the door. If someone answered, then I asked directions to a friend's house—'I'm looking for Ronny Klein's place'—or something like that. If no one came to the door, I let myself in. First thing I did was open up a window toward the back of the house. That way I had an escape route if someone came home. Then I moved quickly through the house, keepin' an eye out for cash, food, and jackets or shoes that might fit me: then I got out as quickly as I could. For months I got away with this. I was never caught at it.

"During that whole time, the police were searching for me as a missing orphan. They spotted me sitting beneath a park tree one afternoon when most kids would've been in school. They asked about this string of robberies that had been reported in the area, but I wouldn't answer their questions, and they couldn't prove a thing."

He stopped a second, which gave me time to add, "You were a regular Jesse James."

"Yeah I guess so," he laughed. "I wasn't hurtin' anyone, but yeah, I was pretty good at stealin' actually . . ." he took a drag. "You know, every person has a point in their life where they're learnin' the stuff that will become their livelihood, and most don't even know it at the time. Course I stopped stealing after a while, but I was sleepin' in the park, thinking ahead about how to get food and clothing, and really surviving on my own. Most kids would be afraid of all that, but I didn't know enough to be afraid. Think that's when I started learning everything I needed to know to make it in the High Sierra."

I got lost in his comments for a moment, thinking about what that point was in my life. "I like how you put that, Phantom, like each person's experiences are really lessons to prepare them for whatever their future holds."

"Yeah, that's how I see it anyway."

"So did the police take you back to Parkland?" I asked, when I realized he hadn't finished that thought. I glanced again at my watch and saw that I had to get to work.

"No, not this time. This time, I was dropped off at a farm house twenty miles outside of Seattle," he said with a sigh. "I dunno if I have the energy to start on that one today."

"Let's leave it there. I need to head to work." Even if I filed a story past 10 p.m. the night before and had a long night of school board or city council meetings ahead of me, I still got a dirty look from the editors if I walked in past 9:00 a.m.

"OK, hon. We'll get to the good stuff. Have a swinging safari." "You too, Phantom."

On my drive to work, my mind returned to life's routine, making my mental to-do list for the work day and turning up the radio to hear if NPR had any story ideas I could repurpose for the local daily. As my car carried me over the bump of Virginia's Blue Ridge Mountains, I spotted a hiker, as I often did, waiting patiently to cross Harry Byrd Highway to continue on the Appalachian Trail, and my thoughts returned to Phantom.

I hadn't noticed how much I was stressing over how our previous talk ended until I realized how relaxed my shoulders now felt. For the first time in weeks, I believed this was more than me pestering an old man. That it was worthwhile, for both of us.

More than anything, I felt appreciative that this tough mountaineer would let me in on the moments in his life he hated most. Maybe something in him wanted to share that burden with someone else. Maybe he was ready to let someone in.

CHAPTER

Dapping

*(v.) A method of fly-fishing in which the fly skips
or dances across the water.*

THERE ARE TWO KINDS OF HIKERS in this world, as Phantom saw it. Those who saunter along, taking their time to relish the journey, and then those who hike to get some place.

For most of his life, he was the latter. When the mountains were home, his hikes were about getting everything he needed to survive. Logging five to 10 miles a day became the norm as he searched out the best spots to fish, hunt, and trap, always keeping an eye out for materials to make shelters.

His hikes grew even longer in the 1950s when he learned the California Department of Fish and Game was stocking the lakes. They put trout in milk jugs and transported them up the mountain on pack mules, and Phantom would follow those fish from the highest elevation lakes, down through the streams, along Owens River, to the lower lakes, pulling three meals a day out of the water.

Now, he'd noticed his time in Bishop had started to change his style of hiking. It was becoming more about the journey. While slowing down was prescribed after the accident, it did more than just help him rebuild his strength. It gave him a chance to get acquainted with parts of the town he'd never bothered to notice before. He wouldn't admit this aloud, but he now found he'd rather sit a minute longer, swap a few stories, and get to know the people who made the two square miles around him hum. He still made regular stops at Schat's Bakkery, but he also started venturing down Main to catch up with the "sandwich artists" at Raymond's Deli. That's what Phantom came to call them because a couple of the guys were budding graphic designers, and the three of them often ended up talking about art. Phantom showed off some of the touch-ups he'd done to thrift shop paintings, and they shared their latest projects, usually posters advertising the next headliner at Rusty's Saloon.

He swung into Mac's Sporting Goods across the street at least four days a week. During each visit, the conversation with the shop manager played out as if it were scripted: "Howdy there, Ron. How are ya?"

"You know, Phantom, if I were doing any better, it'd scare me. Where they bitin' this week?"

"Everywhere I'm puttin' my line in," he'd brag with a wide grin. Denny's, on the other end of Main, became another one of his favorite haunts. As soon as he pushed through the diner's smudged glass door, he felt like he belonged. The smell of bacon grease and burnt coffee were as welcoming as the servers' greetings.

They all knew his order, so Phantom could expect breakfast in front of him half a minute after he sat down. His favorite waitress, Erica, and manager, José, made a fuss when that article came out in the Register that touched on their favorite customer's exploits. "You're famous," they gasped. Then for a while they joked about a mountaineer special, "Famous mountaineers get free coffee before eleven o'clock. Oh, look at that, you just made it."

He figured they probably needed a friend as much as he did. Mexicans had an even harder time than flatlanders in Bishop, a reality that Phantom hated. He wanted to do all he could to help them out, so he gave them the only thing he really could: fish. It got to a point that he was bringing more food into the diner than he was taking out. He'd pull his limit out of the reservoir or South Lake, clean the fish, and then deliver whatever he couldn't eat to José, Erica, Twyla, Eva, and others. In exchange, the servers would describe the soup or the tacos or the sandwich the fisherman's weekly catch had become.

Phantom came to love his mornings at Denny's. It was on one of these mornings that he had an encounter that reminded him of those days when he was the other kind of hiker: a hiker headed somewhere.

"Erica, I'm telling you, this rainbow trout was the size of a toddler," he was saying.

"Really? The size of my little Rafael?"

"Yes, I'm not kiddin' you," he gulped down the last of his coffee. "I took pictures—they're getting developed now. But I'll prove it to ya."

"All right, I want to see this . . . You want a refill?" "Yes, ma'am."

As they chatted, Phantom noticed a woman staring at him from a booth on the other side of the restaurant. He offered an empty smile and got back to his coffee. He was used to stares. A vocal, white-bearded senior citizen wearing clothes adorned with glitter glue doesn't fit in any scene. But, before Erica had even topped off his coffee mug, the woman had plopped in the booth across from him.

"Hello, ma'am. What can I do for ya?" he asked, searching his memory for who this might be.

"Sierra Phantom?" she asked, her brown eyes studied his face.

And then he recognized her, and he realized she was caught up in 40-year-old memories. "Lauren? Lauren?" "Yes!"

"You're kiddin' me!" They jumped up out of the booth and hugged each other.

"Oh my goodness," she said through tears.

"Whooweee, this is incredible," Phantom added. They looked one another over to see what sort of number time had done on each of them. "I'm just . . . I can't believe it."

They only came out of the moment with a word from Erica. "You want to sit together? I can bring your order here when it's ready, ma'am."

"Yes, please," they answered in unison.

Lauren waved over a young woman who had been sitting with her. "This is my daughter, Lisa. We were just sitting over there, and I heard you talking to the waitress about your glitter flies. Even before I saw you, I knew it was you," she said, her hands doing a lot of the talking. She was just as loud and energetic as Phantom remembered her as a kid. "Wow, you look different and the same all at once."

"Yep," he stroked his beard, "I don't think I had this much facial hair back then."

"How'd you recognize me so quickly?" she asked.

"Well, those big brown eyes, of course. And you don't look like you've aged a day." He exaggerated a bit.

"Yeah right," she laughed. "I just celebrated my fifty-eighth birthday. I still can't quite believe that." She looked up at her daughter, who was standing over the booth with a blank smile, waiting for an introduction. She must've been in her mid-twenties. "This is the mountain man who Grandma Louise knew for years and years."

She lit up, and her mouth hung open half a second. "No way . . . Sierra Phantom? At Denny's?" She pronounced the words slowly and with care as if to convince herself of it.

"Lauren told you about me?" he asked.

"Are you kidding me? You were the star of my bedtime stories as a kid—a man who was as wild and free as the Sierras themselves."

"Hmm, wild and free. I like that," he grinned. "Here, take a seat." "Course, for all I knew, you were just part of my mom's imagination. But here you are," Lisa looked at the message above his shirt pockets: MOUNTAINEER – FISHING GUIDE. "Wow, I'm pretty sure you taught me to fish, by way of my mother," she smiled and nodded. "Really nice to meet you."

"You too, hon. You look just like Lauren when I knew her. Well, a bit older, but it does bring back good memories. When she was about nine or ten, she'd dart up and down the trails like a jackrabbit. She'd run circles around me and Louise on our way to a backwoods fishing hole or to some other adventure."

Lauren rested her chin on her hand in silence, taking in the moment. Then in almost a whisper she said, "Just seeing you, my whole childhood flashes back." She wiped happy tears from her cheeks.

Erica delivered two plates of pancakes and refilled the trio of coffee mugs. And with ease, the three settled into an hour-long conversation. "I'd never seen anyone outside of myself who liked to fish as much as your mother," Phantom told Lisa. Then he turned to Lauren, "I don't think Grandma Louise could even get you to sit for a meal before you were out the door with a rod over your shoulder. You probably would've kept your line in the water all night if she would'a let ya."

"Man, I remember how excited I was as a kid to get up here every summer," she said. "I usually had a bag packed a week before just waiting for school to let out. And you made it all that more magical. I was just completely enamored with the idea that someone could live completely off the land. I still am."

"How long has it been since we saw each other?"

"I don't know, I guess I was in college last time I was up here with Grandma."

Phantom started on his third cup of coffee and shook his head in amazement, "Whew, crazy to think back, isn't it . . ."

LOUISE SPROUL WASN'T LAUREN'S REAL grandmother, but rather a good friend of her parents who became a surrogate grandma of sorts. Lauren insisted her summers be spent in Louise's log cabin, about twenty miles up the mountain from Bishop. She felt more at home there than with her parents in LA. And you'd never guess the two weren't related. Phantom would describe Louise as one of the sweetest women he'd ever known, but as tough as nails when it came to the outdoors— stubborn and determined to live life on her terms.

He first saw her on a lake in the dead of winter sometime in the late 1950s. They were both looking to harvest the next few meals from beneath the ice. Phantom hadn't seen people for a few weeks at that point, so he swore she was a mirage, this little woman walking off the lake with a string of fish.

But after he saw her from a distance a second time, he convinced himself to hike down to greet her. He gave a wave to show he meant no harm, and then he walked right up to her. They both offered the kind of greeting you might expect two loners to mutter to one another.

After going days without speaking to another human, even Phantom was silent, as if his brain needed a reboot.

Louise could relate. She finally grinned and let out a louder than intended, "Hello!"

"What are you doing up here?" Phantom asked, realizing too late that he unintentionally sounded rude, as if he had spotted her jumping the fence into his backyard. He soon found out, though, that he was the newbie.

She ignored his tone and said a sentence or two about living in a little cabin in Benton most of her life. Her kids had grown up and moved away, and now it was just her, she told him. She was a petite woman with a few gray hairs scattered among her long brown ponytail, and she had wrinkles that somehow made her look even tougher. They weren't the wrinkles that come with age. They were the ones that can only be found on survivors: people who had put up with life's toughest conditions and come out even stronger on the other side.

Phantom, then in his late 20s, shared his own brief version of why he had been living up there the past eight years or so. One of his camps was set up a few miles from there, at the base of Trafton Mountain.

"Well, you sound like you've made this place your home. What's your name?" she asked.

"Sierra Phantom." He didn't know if it was because his new name felt rehearsed or if it was because of her reaction—"Well, sounds like the range has got their very own mascot"—but either way, he felt the need to explain. "It's sorta pokin' fun at the rangers. They caught wind that I was living around here, and they've been on a hunt tryin' to find me ever since. But I move camps all the time and never leave a trace, so they're outta luck."

He wasn't quite ready to share the real story behind his name. It was really inspired by a comic book series he liked to read as a kid. The Phantom was a muscular guy in purple tights who fought crime. He didn't have much in the way of supernatural powers, but he relied on his strength and intelligence to help the underdogs. Sierra Phantom—John P. Glover—liked that about him.

"What do people call you?" he asked.

"I'm Louise Sproul," she offered a grin and a firm handshake. "You can call me Louise Sproul, Sierra Phantom."

Louise and Phantom became good friends. He'd drop by her cabin to check up on her. They'd walk into town together to get their own sets of supplies, or they'd get in a day of fishing. Then they'd go back to living on their own until one of them needed more than the animals to talk to.

Louise was a real pioneer woman, Phantom always thought. She got along just fine without electricity. She drank water from a well and chopped her own wood. Her favorite place to be was at her wood-fired stove, kneeling to stoke the tinder to just the right temperature to bake her homemade bread. She was the image of what the High Sierra once was, a life that felt so far away to Phantom all these years later. Until he found himself sitting in a Denny's across the table from Lauren, who was now about the same age Grandma Louise was when he first met her.

"So, what's on the schedule for you two while you're in town?" he asked, coming back to the present.

"Guess." Lauren smiled and crossed her arms.

"Hmm, I picture you comin' all this way to spend vacation in a day spa. There's a new one right down Line Street. You'll love it."

"Ha ha, Phantom," she said flatly, returning the sarcasm. "We're here to fish. Do you know anyone who knows anything about how to catch a damn fish around here?"

"Why don't you stop in one of these sporting goods stores. They'll let you in on all the secrets for only three easy payments of a hundred dollars," he joked. "It's a limited time offer, girls. What do you say?"

"I say we kidnap you as our fishing guide for the week," Lisa chimed in. "Your meals are on me," Lauren interjected.

"Sounds like a deal."

CHAPTER

Bendo

*(n.) The bend in a fishing rod when a fish pulls
at the end of the line.*

───────

"ALRIGHTY, FOLLOW ME. Watch your step." He led the pair single file across the narrow top of the South Lake dam. He'd always thought the dam looked like a concrete tightrope stretching from one mountainous ridge to another. Lauren and Phantom almost skipped across the thing in pure joy of being there together, like the old days.

"Hold on a second," he whispered. He put out his hand to tell them to stop, and then he directed them to turn and face the lake with him. "Look at this place."

There they stood, half of South Lake to their left and half to their right. Smooth-faced chunks of granite climbed each side of the basin around them to end in jagged peaks. Trees with brilliant red, orange, and yellow leaves dotted the shore opposite them in the first days of fall. All of it glowed under a pink-orange light, the kind you can only catch during the first seconds of sunrise. As if one of these scenes wasn't enough, the lake, without another soul on it, repeated it all in a reflection. It felt as though they were standing in the palm of Mother Nature's hands, Phantom thought.

"Moorrnin'," he yelled out to her. The words skipped across the calm water and gave Lauren and Lisa a jolt. "Woke ya up, didn't I?" He gave Lauren a friendly jab. "That might'a spooked a couple of fish, too, but I don't care this morning. I want you two to take all this in while you're here."

They smiled and looked out over the lake a minute longer before continuing their careful steps across the dam. When the concrete ran out, they climbed down twenty feet of boulders to reach the water.

"You still doing this?" Lauren asked, sliding her rump across the rocks. "Why, at your age, do you have to pick the most difficult fishing spot to get to?"

"Keeps the crowds out, doesn't it?" "Well, I s'pose that's true."

They each found a spot along the boulders that gave them enough room to cast without crossing their lines. For the next hour they kept words to a minimum, not wanting to pollute the first sacred moments of the day with whatever they had to say. They took turns casting, pulling in several trout, throwing some back, and holding on to a few. It kept on like that until Lisa started the day's conversations.

"So you really lived up here, huh?" she asked, casting her line with ease as though she'd fished alongside her mother all her life.

"Yes, ma'am. Came up here when I was even younger than you, about twenty-one," he began his usual one hundred-word, one hundred-miles per hour spiel. "Built all these camps all over the High Sierra. Actually, the very first one was just up there about a quarter mile." He pointed to a ridge on the opposite side of the lake. "It really was the life. Then one winter I got hypothermia—almost died right then and there—so I had to move into an apartment in Bishop."

"That must've been kinda weird."

"What's that?" he flung his line like a horsewhip along the water. "Living in a town all the sudden after being surrounded by this—all this," she looked around and waved her arm in the air as if to present it to him once again.

"Well, I'll tell ya the truth, I make it up here a couple times a week, and it's still not enough. But I'm tryin' to make the best of living in town— Hey, lookie there. See those big guys swimming there?" He pointed to two large trout hanging out next to the dam.

"Drop your line over there," Lisa said.

Just as Phantom started reeling in to recast, he got a gentle tug on his line. It was a trout about half the size of the two swimming near the dam. "Well, he won't do for dinner, will he?" He unhooked him and set him back in the water before resecuring a glitter fly on the line. "So Lauren, what line of work you in? I always figured you'd grow up to be a park ranger or something."

She smiled and looked over her shoulder, "I don't have a desk job, so I figure that's a small triumph in today's world. Actually, Lisa and I started a rescue farm that takes animals that nobody wants anymore. We see a lot of pit bulls and Rottweilers and a lot of older animals that are never going to be placed. It's called Sacred Animal Sanctuary."

"You always had a way with animals." He laid down his rod and sat on the boulder closest to her. "I remember your eyes growing as big as saucers hearin' about me feeding deer during some of the bad winters up here."

"Yeah, we were kindred souls from the start," she said, taking a second to smile in his direction before getting back to her line. "I was just growing sick of hearing about how many animals are dropped off at shelters and euthanized. I figured, we've got space. Why not? We're on a big ranch outside of Eugene. Very rural." "Wow, hon, sounds nice."

"The next thing we're working on is turning part of the farm into a home for abandoned and abused girls. My background is in therapy, so I've worked with some of these teenage girls who just need a place where they can get back on their feet."

"We've thinking about how we always need help on the farm and how these girls need a safe place, so why not marry the two?" Lisa chimed in.

"Wow, girls. That's great. Doesn't surprise me a bit that you're helpin' those no one else thinks to care for."

"Do you work, Phantom?" Lisa asked.

He laughed a little. "Well, most my work feels more like play. I got my fishing guide business, which is goin' great." He grabbed his rod and eyed the water near the dam again looking for those big trout.

"So you think Bishop finally knows what they have in you?" Lauren interjected.

"What's that?"

"I'm just saying, they better appreciate you; that's all."

"I think they do. There's still some locals around who I've known for a long time, ya know, from coming down the mountain all those years. I got a couple of gals who took care of me after my accident. And there are a couple of high school boys who stop by the bakery most days just to say 'hey.' They're nice boys. But one of the guy's old man is a game warden, and I hear he doesn't like me running my little guide operation without his blessing."

"Man, I believe it," Lauren shook her head. "Bishop's not what it used to be. Didn't you used to help out the game wardens up here?"

"Oh yeah," he said, his voice growing louder. "April 1982, when we got that huge snowstorm, I helped the rangers rescue a whole canyon full of backpackers and fishermen. I got hypothermia and frostbite and the whole deal."

"See, that's what I'm talking about," she said.

"They never liked me living up here all those years, though."

"I just feel like the culture up here has gotten further and further away from its roots, ya know. I used to go into Schat's and get 'hey, Lauren, how are ya? Can we throw in an extra pastry?' Now you go in, shit, they don't know their customers from Adam. Too many to get to know."

He nodded along because he knew she was mostly right. When Phantom and Lauren's Grandma Louise were in their prime, cowboys and mountaineers weren't fodder for movies but undeniable survivors. They knew how to thrive in conditions that a lot of these flatlanders would crumble under, Phantom thought to himself. Now, the markings of tourists coming through Bishop had become noticeable, with its chain restaurants, crowded campgrounds, and flashy signs promising "genuine mountain adventures."

"Yes, ma'am," he finally said with a nod, "it's a different place now." As he thought through all this, his eyes caught Jared Smith waving from across the lake. He and a few others were hurrying to get the resort's boats ready for the day's customers. Jared's family bought the ninety-year-old Parchers Resort a few years back, and they'd done their best to keep it as they had found it. They gave a few of the cabins a facelift but held on to the name, after original owner and newspaperman W.C. Parcher. They kept the operation small, just big enough to share their love of fishing with a few other families at a time.

Phantom let out a gentle laugh and gave a big wave over his head back to Jared, and then he looked back at Lauren. "Some days you can spot some of that old Sierra culture—"

"Oh man, here we go," she interjected. Before Phantom had finished the thought, Lauren got a firm tug on her line. She took a stance atop the boulder as if she were set for a tug-of-war contest. She said through gritted teeth, "Let's pull this guy in."

"Whew, it must be big," Lisa said. The three searched the water where the line disappeared.

"This is why I like this spot," Phantom started. "The fish gather in this corner, nestled up against the dam here—There it is!" A good-sized trout threw itself above the water, shattering the smooth surface. Lauren bent her knees, gripped her reel, and with a steady cadence wound in the line.

"Good, Lauren," the old fisherman encouraged. "Keep it up. Here it comes."

"You're reeling in dinner, Mom," Lisa added.

As she dragged the fish toward shore, Phantom grabbed his net and waited. She gave the handle another stiff turn and lifted the line from the water enough to reveal a rainbow trout that looked as though it couldn't weigh less than five pounds.

"Come on, man," Lauren, out of breath, directed the fish to cooperate. One final tug and Phantom grabbed the line to lift the fish out of the water. He scooped it up just as Lauren's arms collapsed in exhaustion.

"Woo wee," he shouted. "Look at this guy! Hell of a catch."

"It's the glitter flies," Lauren yelled, high on adrenaline. "These things are unbelievable. Ever since I started using them, I've been outfishing everyone. Well, except you."

He gave her a pat on the back, "You're doing somethin' right." After taking a few photos and going on about Lauren's technique, Phantom got back in position along the boulders to try to outdo her. He studied the crystal clear water by the dam looking for that pair of trout again and gave a hard cast that direction.

"Come on now, boys," he whispered.

Lisa sat on a boulder near him, watching him cast and looking deep in thought. After a few minutes, she tried to pick up their conversation where they'd left off. "I see why you'd wanna live up here. It's so peaceful." She took in a deep breath. "But I don't think I could live alone for that long."

He offered a half smile with a polite nod and returned his attention to his line.

"How'd that work? Did you go down the mountain to see friends or family on occasion?"

"No," he quickly blurted the words out, then tried to soften his tone by adding, "not really."

"Well, what do ya mean? Didn't you have anyone you missed? I can't imagine there was no one that—"

He kept his eyes on the fly doing his stroke through the water. "Lisa," Lauren snapped from thirty yards away.

"I didn't mean to—" she looked at her mother then at Phantom.

"No, it's OK," he hollered back to Lauren and said softer to Lisa, "I had a tough childhood, grew up in orphanages and foster homes. So I didn't feel like I was leaving much behind."

Lisa grabbed her rod and returned to her spot along the shore just long enough to catch a small brook trout. She unhooked it, returned it to the water, and then made her way back near Phantom. She pulled a granola bar from her jacket and watched him cast a few minutes until she got the courage to say softly, "Can I ask you something . . ." She paused and looked toward her mother, who was busy tying a fly on her line. As if she had been mulling over the question for the last hour, she said, "What happened to your family?"

Phantom's right hand, which had been gently reeling in his line, paused in place.

Lauren heard and looked up from her project. "Phantom, you don't have to answer that."

The fisherman's stare stayed on the end of his line as his mind ran through possible answers. He took in a lungful of cool Sierra air and let it out slowly. His eyes wandered to the opposite side of the lake where he had set up his first camp almost sixty years earlier, when he was just a tough kid feeling safe for the first time in his life. That version of him would've clocked anyone who asked what he was running from. But standing there with Lauren and Lisa, the question felt surprisingly welcomed. They were the closest thing he had to family, and Lauren was one of the few people who'd lived part of his story with him.

"Sorry, now I'm prying." Lisa grabbed her rod and stood up. "Let's just keep hunting for that golden trout."

He looked down at his reel and turned the handle again to bring in the line. "Lauren, did I ever tell you why I came up here to live?"

"What?" she asked; her attention had returned to her next catch. "Do you know why I moved up here?"

"All Grandma Louise ever told me was you were in World War II and wanted to get as far away from all that as possible. I guess as a kid I pictured you like Mowgli in the Jungle Book, born and raised in the wild."

"Ha ha, yeah, I think I like that version better."

Lauren brought her line in, and Lisa sat back down. And Phantom continued, "But as a kid, I never really knew who I was. All I knew was the bit of information held in a manila folder that followed me from orphanage to orphanage: I was born John P. Glover at St. Joseph Hospital in Orange, California, on July 20, 1926. But even that stuff didn't carry much meaning, ya know? Not without knowing the people who gave me the name. At the orphanages you weren't a name. You were a number."

Before he knew it was coming, he felt a tear drip down his right cheek. He quickly shook his head to move the moment along before the girls noticed. "Anyway, I always just assumed that my parents had abandoned me. There were a lot of kids who were given up during the Great Depression by families who just couldn't afford to feed them."

"You mean, they didn't give you up?" Lisa asked. Now all three of them were sitting on the boulders. Lauren tossed Phantom and Lisa each an apple from her backpack.

"No, I found out later that they'd been killed. I was almost relieved to find out."

Lisa's eyebrows raised.

"Sounds awful saying that, but all I mean is it meant they didn't abandon me. When I was about nineteen years old, I found some German relatives through the nuns at one of my first orphanages. As soon as they gave me the phone number for this family, I dropped everything. I later found out they were second cousins with my father. Anyway, I took a bus from San Francisco to meet them in Los Angeles. For two full days I sat with them and rattled off every question that had plagued me for years. They answered what they could and told me all they knew about my parents."

He paused just long enough to smile toward Lauren. He raised his eyebrows and said quietly, "They sounded pretty great.

"Their names were Eric and Heidi Glover. My father was a German lens specialist, and my mother was an aspiring actress. Just after they got married, they moved from Germany to Hollywood a couple years before I was born. There were a lot of good Germans moving to the United States at that point, tryin' to escape the trouble that was beginning to stir with Hitler coming to power. My father got a job working on lenses in the film industry, and my mother hoped to land a role in a movie with the big timers. 'Bout the time they got settled in their new country, I was born.

"My parents wrote relatives back in Germany off and on. Guess they tried to avoid going on about the palm trees, the beaches, the celebrities and all that. They kept conversation to their new baby boy," he smiled just slightly. "The letters my parents got from family in Germany, on the other hand, were downright scary. The Great Depression hit just as hard in Germany as it did here. The country depended on these short-term loans from the U.S., and once those loans were recalled, Germany was left in bad shape. And, the worse part of it, the Nazis saw people's suffering as their chance to take over. Hitler's storm troopers were slaughterin' entire families to take their land. He sold everything he could get his hands on and used the money to build the army.

"In one of the letters, my relatives told my parents they had heard the troopers were inchin' closer to their farm. They hoped it was just a rumor. But my father couldn't read another word of it without doing somethin' to help. So he and my mother decided to go back to Germany and move the family to California with us. They asked friends to watch me for a couple weeks while they were gone.

"They made it to the farm and started packin' everything up. But the day after they got there, troopers ransacked the place. They killed everyone . . . including my mother and father."

"Oh, I'm so sorry, Phantom," Lauren added softly.

He continued, "By this time, the depression had hit LA real bad. So my parents' friends who now had this three-year-old kid to care for couldn't afford to fill another stomach. They drove me to the Department of Social Services and handed me over to the state. That's how I was told the story, anyway."

The three stayed quiet a few seconds. "Phantom, it sounds like your parents loved you," Lauren added softly. "Loved you enough to protect you."

"Somethin' made me think that . . ." He paused and started again slowly, ". . . that after I was told about my parents, the memory of them would suddenly return. You know, like when you swear you haven't seen a certain movie before, but twenty minutes into it you realize its familiar, and all at once the entire storyline rushes back to you. But that never happened for me." He cleared his throat, and his tone grew louder, "It turns me sour talkin' about all this."

He returned to the moment and looked over at Lauren and Lisa with another half smile and polite nod.

"Sorry, Phantom," Lisa said. He wasn't sure if she was apologizing for his history, or because she'd asked about it. "I didn't know your background or anything."

"Anyway, that's why I love this place," he interjected. He stood up to balance again on the wet boulders and looked across the lake to now spot three or four fishing boats in the distance. "All this. This is my comfort. I always considered Mother Nature my family. She still is."

Lisa and Lauren both followed his lead and stood. "Now, let's get back to it," Phantom said. "Lisa, we're not going 'til you get your big catch."

"I'm on it," Lisa smiled, and she returned to her spot along the shore. For the first time since Phantom had known her, Lauren didn't know what to say. She put her hand on his shoulder and offered a quiet smile, her eyes looked like they were holding back tears. He returned the smile and failed at fighting off a couple of tears that slid down his sunburnt cheeks.

"You're the kindest soul I know; you know that?" he said, handing her fishing rod to her.

"Oh you think so," she said with a teasing grin and a sniff. "Well, that doesn't mean I'm letting you walk away with the biggest catch of the day." "You kidding me?" he grabbed his rod. "I'm just getting warmed up."

They navigated the rocks back to their spots along the shore and cast the rest of the day away.

CHAPTER

Shoaling

(v.) Describes the behavior of fish which aggregate together for the purpose of survival.

WINTER HAS A WAY of slowing life down. Maybe it's God's idea of getting his creation to rest and recalibrate their lives, but for Phantom it was always a season that kept him on edge.

Living in the wild, each year's first snow marked the end of what he thought of as an extended fishing vacation. The start of those long winters brought that back-to-work feeling. Time to prepare, even overplan, for the months ahead. As soon as enough snow fell, he'd build a snow pit like an igloo. He'd fish and trap as much as the weather allowed, and then he would bury everything in what he pictured as a makeshift refrigerator. Between gathering food and boiling water for drinking, he'd hunker down in his own state of hibernation.

Even now in an apartment not much larger than that igloo, his instinct still had him making sure his pantry shelves were stocked. He kept an eye out for coupons and ran out to buy enough canned food to last him three years' worth of winters. He found such a good deal on cans of creamed corn one afternoon it took two trips on the Huffy to get them all back to his apartment. Between snowfalls, he snuck out to get in a few days of fishing on the reservoir. Then he would return to the apartment, eating, sleeping, surviving.

Since he moved down to Bishop, he quietly marked each winter like an anniversary. Another year since he was a man of the wild. Another year in an apartment. Another year on Social Security. This was the first winter something felt different. Good different, he'd say.

His reunion with Lauren lifted his spirits and got him looking for glimpses of the Bishop from her childhood. The Bishop where Joseph's was the only grocery store, and the man who greeted Grandma Louise and Phantom after their long walks into town was Doug Joseph himself. When flatlanders were still just weekend visitors, and the Paiute Indians held the respect of most everyone in the valley because, as Phantom put it, "We knew better then."

Lauren left the retired mountaineer feeling like he carried some sort of responsibility to hold onto, or even revive, the character of the place. The night before she and Lisa left town, they had a run-in with a group of bikers that almost had Lauren convinced to never return.

While the three were waiting in line to order, something shoved Phantom from the back. His right boot slammed down on the hardwood floor in time to catch his balance. "Hey, what's the big idea…" He turned around to see three pair of narrow eyes scowling down at him.

"Here's that dude who peddles his cheap crap at the bakery," the largest of the three spewed. He looked like the classic bad guy in a kid's cartoon. Big, tattooed arms crossed over a black skull on his T-shirt, and a spiked Mohawk exaggerated his height.

"Back off," the skinny old man stepped toward him and spit the words back at him.

"Who's this famous Sierra Phantom?" he flicked the words etched on Phantom's jacket. "I heard about you, telling all these tall tales. You think you're hot shit. But I think you're just full of shit."

Lauren stepped in between the two and enunciated through clenched teeth, "You have no idea who you're talking to. This guy's one of the last living mountaineers."

"Wooo, is that so?" the hefty creature rocked back on his steel-toed boots and grinned at his buddies.

"You don't know a goddamn thing about surviving up here," Lauren hissed, and looked him up and down. "Look at you?"

At that, Phantom grabbed her arm and pulled her away from the muscled trio. "Come on, Lauren. Let's go get that barbecue."

"You don't have a right to kiss his feet," she yelled back at them before reluctantly marching to the table Lisa had strategically chosen on the opposite end of the restaurant. She plopped down in a wobbly chair as old as Phantom and shook her head in disgust. "Ugh, these flatlanders," she huffed. "This is what I'm talking about, Phantom. It's not the same place. And you're just letting 'em get away with talking to you like that."

"They don't deserve a minute of our time," he sighed.

She shook her head and bit her lip. Phantom exhaled to calm himself down. "Ah, Lauren," he gently touched her arm. "Honestly, I'd rather spend time on people who care about this place, like these kids I take on hikes. I was showing a group the other day how to spot edible berries and how to use tree sap to treat blisters and burns. Knowledge is proof, Lauren. I don't got enough energy to convince skeptics."

They worked to keep the rest of the night's conversation to the beef brisket and who had the best catch of the week. It wasn't until the next morning that Lauren again broached what'd been on her mind. Just before she and Lisa pulled out of town, she left her childhood hero with quite the commission: "When we get back here next year, I wanna be able to recognize this place." She leaned on the steering wheel of her Subaru and turned her brown eyes up at Phantom, who was standing beside the car in the Schat's parking lot.

"Well, Schat's still has the best goodies around, doesn't it?" he digressed, and then he handed her a white paper bag full of pastries. "Snacks for the road." He bent down to wave at Lisa in the passenger's seat, "Bye, hon. It was so nice to get to know ya. Take care of your mother, would ya?"

"Of course," Lisa promised with a smile. "We'll be back soon."

Lauren continued, "I'm serious, Phantom. Keep doing what you're doing . . ." He squatted down to meet her at eye level. "Don't worry about what anyone else says, including that game warden. Someone's gotta remind people what the heart of this place looks like. Otherwise there won't be much to preserve before long."

He grabbed her hand and gave it a squeeze. "We'll see you two soon." "Yes, soon," Lisa yelled over them, her feet now on the dash in road trip mode.

"OK, see ya," Lauren waved while the car rolled into motion.

"Have a swinging safari," he shouted as the car turned onto Main Street toward Oregon. Before the Douglas pine on their license plate was even out of sight, he missed them.

But Lauren's words carried him through the winter, and got him that much more antsy for spring. By the time March came, he was ready to bud right along with the flowers.

KNOCK, KNOCK, KNOCK . . . knock, knock, knock. . . "Come on, Paul, Norma, Monte! Get out here, Caren. I've got a surprise for you guys." Within half a minute, Phantom had knocked on every one of his neighbors' doors. It was 7:00 a.m., but he couldn't wait any longer.

Minutes later a groggy figure stood in each of the doorways, some with coffee mugs, others yawning. One, named Paul, wore a heavy scowl as he grumbled, "What's the big idea, man?"

They all faced the courtyard, where Phantom stood in the center with a sweaty bandana wrapped around his forehead and muddy jeans tucked into cowboy boots; he was as excited as a kid on Christmas morning. He'd nagged Elizabeth, the apartment manager, since he moved in to let him put in a garden. "She finally said, 'Yes,'" he announced. Then he waved his arms to present a raised garden bed he was a few hours in to crafting. "Ta daaaa!"

He pointed to a pile of supplies he had hauled back on his bike the night before from two Kmart trips: a bag of dirt, seeds, a few herb plants, work gloves, hand shovels, and cages for their future tomatoes to climb.

"So you're building a garden?" Janet from #18 asked, squinting in the morning sun through her thick glasses.

"We're building a garden—together," he corrected her with a grin. "Here," he handed each of them a pair of gloves and spouted his plan two hundred words a minute. "It will be a community garden. I'll watch over the difficult things, like what to plant and where. But we can all take turns watering, weeding, and enjoying the fruits of our labor."

"OK, OK," said Paul, who was still in his navy bathrobe, and then he dryly added, "but I wouldn't have minded if you'd waited to tell me this a coupla hours from now."

Phantom patted his back, "OK, get some coffee, put on some work clothes, and get back out here. We've got a lot to do."

They all disappeared behind their doors. Phantom took a few minutes to survey the courtyard to finalize his vision for the garden while he sipped on his own mug of caffeine. Minutes later, with no sign of his neighbors, he thought he might be on his own. He figured they had all turned down yet another invitation to live a moment in the fresh air.

He'd tried to get them out for months, offered to take them fishing or even find them a cheap thrift store bike. But there was always an excuse to turn down any adventure, no matter how small. They were either just getting over an illness, just forging into a new one, or just plain tired. It was as if most of them had surrendered to that mysterious stage that hovers somewhere between the last years of life and death.

"Guess that's it," Phantom mumbled to himself. He lit a smoke and started throwing the shovels, seeds, and other supplies back into the plastic Kmart bags.

"I can help ya finish up that bed," he heard Paul say from the doorway of #6.

"Oh, hey, Paul. OK great. It might just be us today." As he finished the thought, doors #10 and #4 opened.

"Can I help, too?" Steven asked in his soft-spoken manner.

"Oh yeah, Stevie." Phantom handed him a shovel. "We need your help, man." With a wordless smile, Steven offered Phantom a slow and gentle high-five as he did most mornings.

Paul set his thrift store radio on a chair and tuned it to KBOV 1230AM to get everyone's energy up. AC/DC blared through the cheap speakers. Paul and Phantom nodded their heads to the beat, and Steven followed their lead.

"Yeah, good stuff, huh?" Paul yelled over the speakers.

By the end of the song, almost every one of Phantom's neighbors stood in the courtyard, eager to get their hands dirty. They had changed out of pajamas and into work clothes, and they each had their new garden gloves in place.

For the first time in a long time, Phantom didn't know what to say. He watched as each of them snapped into action: the guys fetched another bag of soil from his apartment and the women set out supplies.

"Looks like we got beans, cucumbers, onions, beets, tomatoes, and oooh those chilies are gonna taste great," Carmen announced, thumbing through the seed packets. She subtly winked at Phantom, "We'll have a whole produce section here by June." She was just as eager as he was to give their neighbors a reason to get out of bed.

"That's the plan," he said, grinning back at her. "Now, let's get this stuff in the ground."

Phantom assigned each of them a job: Carmen and Janet mixed all-natural plant food into the soil, Monte made small signs out of cut-up cardboard to mark where each type of seed should be planted, and Steven tidied up the courtyard around the garden.

Meanwhile, Paul and Phantom finished putting together the two beds. They built them to form a V shape, so they looked as though they were designed along with the courtyard's shade structure.

Once he had the four people standing in front of him who seemed most excited about planting, he offered a pep talk. "Now, you can't just throw seed on the ground and hope something comes of it," he instructed. "You've got to water it. You've got to nurture it. You've got to gently guide it the way you want it to go."

They nodded along, and then each took their stance at different sections of the box. As if they felt personal responsibility for the job they'd been charged with, they performed every step with slow care. They dug small holes, gently tapped the seed packets to let one or two tiny seeds drop to the bottom, then covered it with a blanket of dirt. They painstakingly repeated this process until one of those not involved in the planting finally griped, "How ya comin' over there?"

"Done!" Steven announced several minutes later as he leveled off the dirt over his last planted seed.

"Whew, looks good, doesn't it?" Phantom encouraged. Steven nodded in agreement. "Stevie, you wanna bring over that hose and give everything a good drink?"

Elizabeth surprised the work crew with sandwiches from Raymond's Deli to cap off the day. "I don't know why I didn't let you do this earlier," she admitted to Phantom quietly while everyone snacked and looked over the final product.

"Ya know, hon, all that matters is that we're powering forward with it now," he smiled and rocked back on the heel of his boots.

Then she yelled to the group, "Hey everybody, gather around the garden. Let me get a photo." She ran to the apartment office, then emerged with a camera. "OK, now, everybody say . . . let's see, how 'bout . . . green beans!"

"Green beans!" they yelled in unison.

"Looks good," she said. "I think I'll send this to the Register."

They all chipped in to help Steven put the final touches on the courtyard. When Phantom thought Elizabeth was busy in the complex office, emailing the photo to the newspaper, he ripped down the "No Parking" signs that seemed to scream at intruders.

"Hey, how will we keep people from pulling up here?" she demanded a second later, marching out of the office.

"If it looks like a courtyard instead of a parking lot, they'll know not to park here," Carmen replied, saying exactly what Phantom was thinking.

"Well, OK," Elizabeth conceded. "We'll see how that goes."

He handed the crumpled signs to Carmen, who grinned at the small victory and threw them in a black garbage bag that held the rest of the day's trash.

Within the hour, the sun began to sneak behind the peaks beyond Bishop. Most of the day's crew went back into their apartments and, to Phantom's surprise, returned seconds later with jackets and lawn chairs. They found a spot beneath the huge cottonwood, but they didn't look out toward Clarke Street. Without saying a word, they each positioned their chairs with their backs toward the street to face their new garden.

"Whew, you sure know how to get people off the couch," Paul said as he stretched his arms and smiled. "I'm pooped."

"Today was fun," Steven said softly, more to himself.

"Yeah, I won't go on about missing my soap opera," Janet laughed.

They didn't look at one another as they talked but mindlessly stared toward the garden bed as though it were a bonfire holding their attention. "So, how do you know all this about gardening?" Carmen asked Phantom. "Don't tell me you had a garden hidden among the trees up at

South Lake?"

"No, no. My goal up there was to not leave a trace," he laughed. "I learned to garden a long time ago. Guess I was fourteen, fifteen years old."

"You grow up in the country?" Paul asked.

"Well, I moved around a lot—grew up in orphanages mostly. Most were in the city. Except my last place was out in the sticks, outside of Seattle."

"Really, an orphanage?" Paul asked gently, unsure if he was welcome to more details.

"It was a boys' home, a place for teenagers who were either orphans or had gotten in trouble with the law. It was the last place I was in before going out on my own. The man in charge taught all of the boys how to do a little bit of everything. That's where I learned carpentry, too." He paused long enough to take a deep breath of the cool spring air.

He unwedged a cigarette from its pack and joined half the others in forming a tobacco cloud above the courtyard before starting up again, "Yeah, it was pretty ironic, actually. It was the first orphanage where the headmaster—a Mr. James Burton—said, 'Hey, if you wanna run, there's the door.' There were no fences, but it was the only orphanage I never ran from. See, his goal was to teach each of us boys a little bit of somethin' about everything so we would have skills before we were out on our own. He knew we wouldn't learn a thing if we were held there like captives."

"That's how you got so handy, huh?" Elizabeth asked with a smile, gently referring to his first few months at the complex when she let him cover part of his rent by doing odd jobs around the apartments.

"Yeah, that's where I got my start," he said and took a drag on his cigarette. Talking more to himself now, he continued, "You know, Mr. Burton, he really was the first person in my life who showed me I could be good at something. That I was worth something."

Phantom noticed they were each looking up at him as if he'd said something important. They just smiled a second and then went back to their cigarettes and returned their stares to the fresh soil.

Green thumbs

Residents at IMACA's Valley Apartments, together with IMACA's construction crew, celebrate the completion of their new garden space. On Thursday, residents planted tomatoes, chiles, eggplants, cucumbers, onions, beans, beets and radishes. Photo submitted

Rennie at South Lake.

Sierra Phantom's Huffy rests outside of Rennie's mobile home.

Photos by Danielle Nadler, July 2012

Bishop, California

Ron at Mac's Sporting Goods in Bishop.

CHAPTER

Peg

(n.) The element of the story that makes it valuable.

"LOOKIE HERE, WE MADE IT IN THE PAPER! I thought you'd want to see. Talk soon. Until then, have a swinging safari! – Sierra Phantom."

He sent me a newspaper clipping that showed him with a huge grin surrounded by his more subdued-looking neighbors standing proudly in front of a garden. He was much more outlandish looking than I'd pictured, with pants sloppily tucked into cowboy boots, aviator sunglasses, and a bandana holding back his hair as wild and free as he once was. There's no other way to put it: he looked bad ass. Like a character from some indie film. I laughed a little at how much he must stand out in any crowd.

I studied the clipping for a good two minutes. I tried to imagine what the apartments in the background might look like inside and wondered if the neighbors pictured were any of the friends he talked about on occasion. It felt good to hold something he had held just days earlier. As though it was proof that this larger-than-life character, whose stories I'd catch myself daydreaming about, actually existed.

I finally stuck the clipping to the refrigerator and called Phantom. "I see you put your garden in," I started.

"Oh yeah, so you got the picture?" His deep voice chuckled a little at the thought, maybe because he also felt that this exchange of something tangible was welcomed proof he wasn't imagining anything either.

"You know, ever since I moved in, I've been asking the apartment manager if I could put in a garden, and she finally let me do it. And, man, it's going great . . ." he hit his usual stride. "I got my good friend next door, Carmen, doing the watering, and I have a couple other neighbors helping with the weeds. I do some of the trickier stuff like training the green beans and lemon cucumbers to go the way I want them to. Since I don't really got family, I'm callin' these plants my children. I take care of them, nurture them, and make sure their space is clear so they can really take off."

"Sounds like you could teach me a thing or two," I interjected. "My husband and I have a little herb garden, but I'm not very good at keeping up with the weeding."

"That's key, hon, gettin' those weeds outta there," he instructed. "I've always had a bit of a green thumb."

Thinking that might be the chance to steer the conversation to where we'd left it last time, I asked, "Where'd you learn to garden? Or do you just have a natural knack for it? I know a lot of people do."

"Mr. Burton taught us at Green Hill Academy—that was my last orphanage. He showed us all the tricks. Each plant likes things a certain way, ya know, some take more water, some take less . . ."

I let him go on a bit more while I looked at my notes. The last time we talked, he was saying the police found him after he ran away from Parkland and were getting ready to send him to a foster home. "Just a second, Phantom. Can you rewind a little? I don't think you told me about that foster home on the farm. You know, after you ran away, and the police found you."

"I didn't? Hmm," he sounded as if he'd rather keep on with his gardening story. The line was silent for a few seconds until he sighed, "Well, OK, I guess we can go back there." He said this as though we were going to journey through time.

"You said the police found you. Why didn't they send you back to Parkland?" I nudged him along.

I heard another sigh like he had just plopped on the couch. "Think they knew I wasn't going to stay put at Parkland, so they dropped me off at a farm house about twenty miles outside of Seattle. That was always a scary thing."

"What's that?"

"The drive to a new place, not knowing what it would be like. I was a pretty brave kid, but that always got me. 'Cause you never knew how awful it might be; it could be even worse than the last. And this place was one of those that was worth dreading."

I heard the click, click, click of his lighter, and a second later he started again, "These were the type of people who thought they were pretty smart, takin' in as many foster kids as the state of Washington would give 'em. All for a hefty monthly paycheck; think it was more than a hundred dollars, which was a lot of money back then. The mother worked two jobs: one at a diner and one as a cocktail waitress, and the dad was a drunk.

"I was one of six foster kids in that place, and I discovered from day one they wanted nothing to do with us. The mother was all right, but she was never around. And the dad ignored us if he was in a good mood, but, the rest of the time, he was drunk enough to come up with excuses to beat the hell outta us." He stopped as if that was enough to sum up that place, and he was ready to move on.

"So how long were you there?" I prodded.

"Guess it was more than four years in all. I was the oldest. As I grew a little, the dad let me carry his twenty-gauge shotgun. Said I was old enough to take on the responsibility of watching over the place. Well, I'll tell ya, all that really meant it was my neck if anything went wrong.

"One night, the younger boys were roughhousing and dropped a couple of the shotgun shells down the furnace. The shells never went off or anything, but it was enough to ruin the thing. All I remember is waking up to the dad beatin' the hell outta me. So the next night, I ran away."

"Another escape," I whispered.

"Yeah, I was pretty much always thinking up ways to get out of these places, and every chance I got I'd run to the nearest mountain. Out that far from the city, any other orphan would hitchhike to the city, hoping they could rely on handouts. But, to me, nothing felt more like home than standing right smack in the middle of the wilderness," he said, slowing down his words as if to enjoy the moment again.

"Before I escaped the farm, I stole a fishing rod from the barn, and I put it to good use. I tracked streams all the way to Chester Morse Lake and caught enough bass and walleye to keep me from goin' hungry. I didn't have much for warm gear, though. I was too eager to get out of that place and didn't think much beyond the warmer months.

"So after about two months out there, I finally surrendered to the idea that I had to go back to the farm. I figured I'd stay for a few more months, get some equipment together, and come up with a plan to try it again. But, as it turned out, I wasn't there long enough to come up with any plan.

"One day a lady showed up from the Department of Child Services and charged the mother with negligence. I don't know how the state ever found out that the mother was never around and the father drank all the time. Either way, I was glad to get out of there."

He took a deep breath and said softly, "And then that feeling came back again, dreading what the next place might be like. Always made me nervous. When the lady from the state came to the farm, she told the group of us kids to go collect our things and that the state was movin' us. "I remember going into the bathroom and closing the door to pray for the first time in my life. I prayed for a better family this time, maybe even a nice family. Well, we all piled into her car. She dropped the younger kids at Child Protective Services, a large building in downtown Seattle and told me, 'they'll be fine' before starting toward the place I was assigned to."

"Were you sad you weren't going with those other kids?" I asked. He never seemed to talk about other kids.

"Nah, we could never warm up to one another in that mess of a place."

"Hmm," was all I could add. "So where were you taken?"

"Well, I didn't really know why, but she started drivin' me out of the city. She drove and drove until the tall downtown buildings disappeared, then past the suburbs until we were driving through the deep forest near Rainbow Falls State Park. The farther she drove, the more excited I got. I finally asked her, 'So, where we going?' My new home would be Green Hill Academy, she told me. It was a state juvenile detention center, but a few of the kids there were orphans."

His voice softened like he was telling me a secret, "They probably built the place in the middle of nowhere to scare kids into sticking around, but it was on the edge of exactly where I wanted to be.

"The lady parked the car and led me into a small building. I still remember the door held a little sign that read 'superintendent.' Inside, a tall guy who looked like he could have been a linebacker in another life stood up from a desk chair.

"'Hey there, you can call me Mr. Burton.'" Phantom's voice dropped even deeper as he spoke for the man. "In one step, this guy made it to the other side of the desk and offered his huge hand for a shake. 'You must be J.P. Glover?'"

"'Yes sir,' I said, pushing back my shoulders to stand a bit taller. I was surprised by his professionalism toward me, a scrawny orphan who most headmasters considered scum.

"He sat back in his chair and told me, 'You'll notice we have no fences here at Green Hill. You wanna run, there's the door, kid. You wanna straighten up and fly right, we'll help you out, make sure you get a good education and maybe even a promise of some sort of future.'

"Ya know, at first I felt a little unsure about this place. No fences? No consequences for running? What's the catch, ya know? But if this guy was for real, it was the first time anyone had given me a choice. I was fifteen and stealing every chance I got. So right then and there, I decided to straighten up.

"He got a kid about my age named Jerry Hallas to show me around. He told me there were a lot of kids at Green Hill who had gotten in trouble for robberies, drugs, arson, things like that. But he was an orphan like me, so we ended up gettin' along great."

That was the first I'd heard him mention a friend. I stayed quiet, and couldn't help but smile, while my fingers tapped away trying to keep up with him.

"Now, there were different jobs at the academy, and you could choose which ones you wanted to do. If you got tired of choppin' firewood, Mr. Burton would let you try milking cows. When you were tired of that, you could give metal shop a try. Once I got settled, I tried my hand at each of the different jobs. Most of them helped the place operate, but they were also meant to teach us a skill that we could take with us, maybe even turn into some sorta career.

"In one of the rotations, I learned the basics of carpentry. We painted doors, fixed chairs and tables, and built whatever needed building. The place also had a vegetable garden—that's where I learned to garden. I also learned a lot of what I know about fishing from Mr. Burton. Every few weeks, he would take the best-behaved boys camping. He taught us to fly fish and explained some survival basics, like how to start a fire without a match or camp without leaving a trace.

"It turned out to be a pretty good deal. It was the first place I wasn't picked on, and Jerry and I ended up being sort of the comedians of the place."

"Really? What do you mean by that?" I added.

"Well, we organized a group of the funniest guys and put on skits for the rest of the school. It got to be a regular thing. Every Friday night everyone crowded the auditorium to watch, and we kept 'em laughing with these hilarious story lines. I played the piano; Jerry played a guitar; and three others sang."

"Sounds pretty fun," I laughed a little, happy to hear more good news. "Mr. Burton got the biggest kick out of it. He suggested we bring the shows to the Eagles Club, where he was a member. From there, we took the skits to the Shriners, the Elks, and any other group in town we were invited to entertain. Most nights, the groups took up a collection for us just as a thank you. One night, the Masons gave us ninety-five dollars, which was a fortune in those days."

"Oh dang, that's pretty good. What'd you do with the money?"

"Mr. Burton kept just enough to cover gas to the shows, and he let us keep the rest. On our trips into town on Sundays, we'd go get hot dogs or comic books. More than anything though, we really enjoyed performing. I was the biggest clown of all of them," he said loudly, bragging now. "I wrote most the skits and led the act on the piano. There was one skit I can still do from memory. We called it 'Country Boy Goin' to the City,' and it was about a kid who grew up in the sticks. He had never been to a hotel and had never seen electricity, so the city was a big adventure for him. Imagine a few guys playing some twangy tunes in the background while another guy and me take center stage."

"OK," I said, and followed his directions.

He started, "'Be careful now, son,' the dad warned the boy, who I played. 'The city is chock full of dangers.'

"When the boy returned home, he told his dad what he had seen in that great, big city. 'I went to this place called a- a- a- hooo-tel,'" Phantom sputtered in a thick country accent, laying his performance on real thick. "'When I was ready for some shuteye, I tried to blow out this candle in my room. I blew and blew and blew, and it just sat there, shinin' away. So I threw my glass of water on it. That should take care of it. Well, I don't know what that candle stick was made of, but sparks flew every which way.'

"The old men in the audience would slap their knees and laugh until their cheeks turned red," Phantom said and paused long enough to take a drag from his cigarette. "It was great, standing up there on stage making people laugh. It was the first time in my life I closed my eyes and slept great every night."

"That sounds like a pretty good place."

"Oh, yeah. It was. It's the only place worth saying much about," he said, as if he was glad our conversations were past his earliest years. Then he continued, "Now, one afternoon, Mr. Burton walked around the property, calling a few of the boys to come to the wood shop. He gathered about ten guys, including me.

"'This here is Mr. Claudley Hickman,' he said, standing next to a thin man who looked like he was sixty or so by his wrinkles and tired eyes.

"'Hey there boys,' the man said, slowly walking in front of the group and taking the time to look each of us in the eyes. 'I'm told Mr. Burton has some pretty good carpenters out here. Well, I'm looking for an apprentice. I'm going to hang around for the next couple days to see what kind of work you boys do.'

"Mr. Burton divvied up jobs around the place that needed fixin'. We cut boards for shelves, sanded and painted doors, and built a fence around the garden—the first and only fence in the place. My project was to repair a drawer on Mr. Burton's desk, sand the whole desk down and re-stain it.

"'That's lookin' good, kid,' Mr. Hickman told me while I was working on it. He eyed my repair job and pulled open the drawer, which, after my work, smoothly slid along the rail. I grabbed a piece of sandpaper and began scraping it along the faded stain of one of the desk legs.

"'Can I show ya somethin'?' he asked. I shrugged my shoulders in agreement. He took the sandpaper and brushed the desk leg so hard I thought the whole thing would be dust by the time he was done.

"'Feel that. Real smooth, right?'

"I touched the desk leg. It felt like silk.

"'It's tough at first, but the better sand job you do, the better the stain will turn out.'

"So I tried that while he lingered a few minutes and monitored my technique. 'Much better. That should turn out nice,' he said; then he plopped down in Mr. Burton's desk chair. 'Hey kid, what sort of ideas you got for your future? You want to do this kind of work?'

"I hadn't really thought about it much. I'd always liked working with my hands, so I figured carpentry might be a pretty good fit. I told him, 'I like buildin' things.'

"'You've got a talent in this. If you want to come on with me to work in my shop, I'll take ya.'

"So there you have it. From that point on, I was no longer a ward of any state. I was on my own." He took in a deep breath and let it out quickly. "I felt free, ya know?"

In Virginia, I sat quietly on the other end of the line. I didn't really know. I didn't think I'd ever been able to recognize what freedom really felt like because I'd never been without it. Still, I mumbled in agreement before we said our goodnights.

CHAPTER

Jump

(n.) Continuation of a story from one page to another.

THE FREEST I HAVE EVER FELT was after my college graduation. About the age Phantom was when he responded to the allure of the High Sierra, I gave in to a similar pull toward the Golden State.

I'd grown up hearing about the place. Mom and Dad met in Southern California, before moving to Colorado and later to South Dakota, determined, it seems, to inch farther and farther away from the sun. Being raised on the cold Midwestern plains by parents who once lived near Disneyland was one big tease. Subtle mentions from Mom about picking oranges from her grandfather's orchards, or from Dad about Christmas tree shopping in shorts and flip-flops created in me a constant appetite for something more. More people, more shopping, more elevation change, and, most certainly, more sun.

Dad's death my senior year of college only reinforced my longing to move west, to experience this place listed on my birth certificate. Call it an escape, but with a journalism degree in hand, the realization that I could apply for a job almost anywhere excited me, and landing a job at a newspaper on the West Coast sounded like anything but work.

I sent résumés and writing samples to dozens of publications, from as far south as San Diego and as far north as Eureka, but didn't get a single reply. Without so much as an interview set up on the other end of Interstate 15, I packed everything I owned into my Oldsmobile and drove across the country. And, as if it was prompted by my decision to set out in faith, I got my first phone call from a publication minutes after I crossed the Nevada-California border.

The man on the other end of the phone said his name was Eric and he was the city editor at the Tracy Press, a mid-sized daily in the San Joaquin Valley. Less than a week later, I was hired, and I began a job that would teach me more about how to get a good story than all four years of college combined.

This is where I truly began to understand Journalism Rule #3: get out of the newsroom.

Eric felt it was his personal duty to get his new hire out of her comfort zone. His repertoire of assignments included articles on the local surge of meth labs, the gangs that were quietly recruiting high schoolers, and the dangerous racial tension that was worsening among the four thousand inmates in the regional prison. Interviews for stories like those couldn't be done by phone or through email, he told me. You had to grab your notebook and go.

At that point, I had written more articles on county fairs and lemonade stands than crime, but I kept any anxiety I felt to myself. "I got this," I'd whisper to myself, ignoring my sweaty palms and pounding heart as I approached whatever that day had in store. I'm not sure what it was that drove me. Whether a determination to throw off the label of being a naïve Midwesterner, oldest daughter of a preacher, or the terrifying thought of failing at my first job out of college. But I boldly, sometimes blindly, forged into every assignment Eric dished out in our weekly news meetings.

I walked through the city block that locals called Tweaker Hill. I stood in the living rooms of families who'd lost sons to gang violence. I rode along with cops to fatal crashes and drug busts. I sat across a cold, metal table from convicted murderers to hear and see their stories for myself. At one point, I even floated the idea of living on the streets of San Francisco to write an in-depth account of the city's homeless. My mother talked me out of that one.

But those assignments were the first time I experienced the power of stories. I saw that it's stories that make us human and reveal the human in others. They connect people who, just moments earlier, were strangers.

SEVEN YEARS AFTER Eric first tossed me a reporter's notebook, I knew I was failing at the most important lesson he taught me in that musty California newsroom: the stories worth telling are often the most daunting to get, and you've got to step out of your cubicle to get them.

Some days it felt as though we were making progress, Phantom and me. That we were doing something important. And my earliest lessons in the newspaper business acted as a subtle guide in this interview that was unfolding a story like none I'd ever covered. But a lot of days I felt like I was wasting an old man's time, prodding him to revisit years he had worked so hard to escape when, instead, he could be out enjoying his golden years.

Here I was working on a story I sat 2,500 miles away from about a man who lived out this idea that dwelling far from predictability, on the edge of the unknown, is the only way to have a story, a life, worth sharing. Hunched over my laptop late one Sunday night, I tried to piece together an image of Sierra Phantom based on everything he'd told me. I resented the fact that there were so many other things I didn't know about him: his mannerisms, his posture, what his smile looked like, and how often he showed it. It felt impossible to truly understand who he was over the phone.

I shared this frustration with him during one of our routine calls. "I'm enjoying our talks and everything, but I wish we could do this all in person. It'd be so much better to walk around Bishop with you or drive up to South Lake." I sighed, "I don't know . . . it's just tough to know how to do this."

"Well, you're welcome here any time," he said, louder and more welcoming than you'd think a guy of his stature could muster. "We'd have to figure out a place for you to stay, but I got a couple ladies I know who'd take you in."

I had zero vacation time at my current job and didn't have the money for a cross country flight. "Well, for now, let's just keep going," I said, trying to sound more optimistic than I felt.

In my attempt to envision where he was, what he was wearing, what he was doing—who he was—I started asking him the most detailed questions. Questions that would annoy most people, but he didn't sound bothered by them. "So," I said at one point. "What are you doing right now?"

"Well, just sitting on my couch, smoking." "What do you smoke?"

"Paiute cigarettes. They're all natural, so they're really not bad for ya. I get 'em on sale from the reservation, which starts just outside of town."

"Are you drinking anything?"

"Just a glass of water. I've never drank any alcohol or anything." "Never? Why not?"

"I grew up with too many drunks in my life that I never wanted anything to do with it—" he stopped mid-sentence. "Well, now, let me take that back. I drank one time. But man, let me tell ya, it was enough to convince me to steer clear of the stuff."

"Really? Can I hear about that?"

"OK, well, I gotta back up a little. You remember Mr. Hickman, the carpenter I became an apprentice for?"

"Yes," I said.

"Well, I moved with him into Seattle. Now, that was a whole 'nother adventure…"

I smiled and readied my fingers on my computer keys.

"We got to know each other pretty quickly on that drive from Green Hill Academy into the city. He really had experienced some amazing things in his fifty or so years. The type of stuff I wanted to experience. He told me about his years looking for gold in Alaska and Brazil and how he'd find odd jobs to cover his expenses when his searches came up dry. That's how he learned carpentry. When he'd first moved to Seattle, he did carpentry jobs on homes in the suburbs, but he kept gettin' stiffed. He'd charge half of the cost up front and the other half when the job was done, but most of the time customers didn't pay the second half. His friend finally suggested he move his business into Chinatown because the Chinese always paid their bills. He told him, 'The Chinese will starve before they have an unpaid debt.'

"So Hickman packed up his business and turned a small building in Chinatown into a workshop. Not only was he the only white man living in Chinatown, but he was also the only carpenter. At that time, no other whites in the area would work with the Chinese cause they were all prejudiced, which left us plenty of work."

Phantom paused, and I heard the usual click of his lighter, firing up another cigarette.

"At this point, I thought I had a pretty good handle on carpentry, but Hickman was a master at it. I don't think there's anybody else who could've taught me more. He taught me to slow down until I had a knack for it. To not work faster than I was comfortable. That would mean fewer mistakes that I had to return to. In those days, you took a lot of pride in what you did. You wanted to do your best; you needed to do your best, or you'd starve.

"The one hurdle was the language barrier. We'd use hand signals and point to paint samples, or we would draw pictures to try to pick up what customers wanted done."

"That sounds like it'd be tough," I added.

"We usually made do. Well, except for the time a restaurant owner wanted a doorway painted brown, but we thought he meant blue. This other time we built a kitchen table with four chairs when a family had only asked for the table because that was all they could afford. 'Course Hickman let them keep the chairs free of charge.

"After that, he told me, 'We can't keep this up, kid.' So the next day he talked to the man who oversaw Chinatown to see if there were any possibilities of getting translators for cheap.

"The two had become pretty good friends because of all the work Hickman had done around town. 'I have a better idea,' he told Hickman. 'Why doesn't your apprentice learn Chinese?'

"He said he would make sure I was welcomed as the first white kid in a school that taught Mandarin and Cantonese. He figured it would only help his people if Hickman and I could communicate with them. There was a lot of work to be done in that little ten-block district. Hickman pitched the idea to me, making those same points.

"'It's a win-win,' he told me. 'You'll get to learn a new language for free.'

"'Chinese seems impossible,' I said, trying to imagine me rattling off those squirrelly soundin' sentences.

"But he said, 'Well, if we keep this up, we'll paint all of Chinatown pink over some misunderstanding.'"

"So right then and there I agreed to it. I worked all day, and then I would spend the evenings at the Chong Wa Education Society. The Chinese students would go to regular public school all day and then sit through another four hours at Chong Wa. I couldn't believe it.

"The first thing I learned about the Chinese languages is that they are really hard. Even the masters don't know the whole alphabet. There are more than thirty-five thousand characters, and a phrase can be taken a number of different ways dependin' on what octave you speak it in. I ended up really likin' it, though. I never liked school growin' up. It was about doing just enough to get out of any beatings or extra chores. "Now I was back in the classroom again. But this time I had a patient teacher and a clear picture of why all the work was worth anything. I practiced my pronunciations while I worked in the shop, mumbling to myself. In the evenings, Hickman quizzed me on phrases from the textbook. And within about six months, I knew enough that I could pick up the basics for customers' orders. I always had to ask them to speak very slowly. And they would. I think they appreciated a white kid willing to learn their language, and a tough language at that.

"My favorite part about the whole thing was testing out my new skill at the restaurants, though it was still a bit shaky. Hickman paid me plenty, maybe even overpaid me, so I had money to try out this new world of cuisine. It was great. Almost every day I'd try some place different, Chinese, Japanese, Portuguese, Korean, or Filipino food. It was like nothing I'd ever experienced before. So much of my life food had been just slopped on a plate as a means to get rid of hunger. No longer from that point on. To this day when I eat, I don't just do it to stop feeling hungry, but I really want to experience the taste, ya know?"

"Yeah, for sure," I added.

"Now, here's the drinking story," he offered as a teaser. "At this point, I was almost in shock that I could do whatever I wanted to do. When I was done with my day's work, I had time of my own, so I made a few friends. One of the older students I was friends with at the Chinese school invited me to a party one night. He told me to meet him outside the school, and he would drive us to the place a few miles from Chinatown. Well, the guys at the party kept handing me these glasses of Coke, and it tasted pretty good to me, so I kept drinking them. By the time I realized the drinks were spiked, the guy who brought me to the party had left, and I was too dizzy to try to figure out why.

"I think I mumbled somethin' like, 'Just point me in the direction of Chinatown,' to one of the girls.

"She sorta giggled and faced me toward the lights of downtown. 'Head that way.'

"I don't remember exactly how I got home, but Hickman told me the next day that it took me fifteen minutes just to get up the stairs to our apartment. He didn't bother to help because he was gettin' too much of a kick out of it."

He stopped a second to laugh. "Once I was inside, I slammed the door behind me. A shoe went flyin' one direction and my jacket another, and I passed out on the couch. Oh, and the next morning, was I sick as a dog!"

I laughed along with him.

"The sun came through the window blinds, resurrecting me just enough to feel the pain that had taken over every inch of my body. My head pounded so hard at my temples I could hear it. My stomach felt like I had been poisoned, and every limb felt too heavy to lift. So I repositioned my pillow and dropped my head like a bowling ball, vowing half-consciously to sleep through this torment.

"Then I heard Hickman from the kitchen, 'Time to get up, kid.' He was crackin' eggs and humming a much too upbeat song for such a morning.

"'Ohhh!' I wailed in pain.

"He asked, 'So what happened to you?'

"I remember just looking up at him blankly. There was no need to explain. Hickman liked a drink himself. Really, he probably drank too much. He did it as a pain reliever. See, he worked with lead paint for so long when nobody knew it was poisonous. It left him with a lot of stomachaches, so he drank to keep down the pain. He never got mean when he drank, though, just quiet.

"'Remember, you've got that job with Ms. Lin,' he reminded me and grabbed my shoulder sorta sympathetically. 'Sorry, bud. You still gotta do the job.'

"'Ugghhhh,' I moaned, holding my stomach at the thought of moving, let alone working. Hickman brought me a piece of toast and a glass of water, said it would make me feel better. I eyed that toast for the next few minutes. Finally gaining my bearings, I took two or three bites, pulled on my jeans, grabbed a bucket of stain from the shop, and walked to the job. I was pretty upset most of the morning, but by the afternoon I felt a little more myself, and I left Ms. Lin with a beautifully stained front door.

"Looking back now, I respect Hickman for what he did. I was a pretty good kid at that point, but I think he wanted to make sure I stayed that way." Phantom paused a moment and softened his tone. "I think that's what a father would have done. It was a lesson in being a man of your word." He took a puff from his cigarette. "Hickman was the closest person I ever had to a parent."

He stopped, so I asked, "Did you stay in touch with him?"

"Oh yeah, a little. After I left for the war, we wrote letters off and on. But I later heard he died just a couple years after I left."

"Hmm, he really sounds like a great guy," I added, for what it was worth.

"Yeah," Phantom sounded like he was smiling. "His going on about 'the golden rule of carpentry' really stuck with me. If you're going to do something, do it right. Otherwise, what's the point? Your hands are creating this, so take pride in it, ya know?"

I nodded and smiled, as if he was sitting across the kitchen table from me.

"Looking back now, I lived by those words the rest of my life," he said softly, then added with a laugh, "and I'll tell ya, I haven't touched an ounce of alcohol since."

CHAPTER

School

(n.) A group of fish swimming together.

"JUST KEEP PEDALING," the mountaineer thought to himself. Push down with the right, now the left, right, left, right, left . . .

The pace picked up, and he kept the wheels spinning until they carried him to Pleasant Valley Dam Road. He turned right and headed toward the reservoir. After a busy June and July spent keeping up with requests for tours, he was taking a day for himself.

A few hundred feet past the turn, he got off the Huffy to catch his breath. He let out a wheezing "Whewiee . . ." a breathless admission of exhaustion to only his shadow, which was cast against a brittle desert shrub as thirsty as he was. He took a long drink from his water jug and convinced himself that pushing the Huffy up the last stretch of road would save some energy to reel in a big trout. Just as he began his walk along the road's shoulder, he heard the rumble of an aging pickup truck at his back.

"Sierra Phantom?" he heard from the driver's seat as the rusty Chevy pulled to a stop. The morning sun hit the windows just right so Phantom couldn't see who was yelling at him. "Hey, you want a ride?"

The window rolled down, and Phantom peered in to see Travis, son of the fish and game warden. "Oh, howdy there," he said, grinning in an attempt to hide his exhaustion. "Yeah, if you could take me this last stretch, it'd give me more time on the water."

"Yeah, for sure." He hurried out of the driver's seat to help Phantom lift his bike into the truck bed. "So, you're fishing at the reservoir today?"

Phantom pulled himself up to the passenger seat and didn't bother to buckle the seatbelt. "Yeah, looking forward to a quiet day on the water. Thanks for the ride. I think it's this emphysema that's slowin' me down." He snuck in an extra deep breath. "Ya know, I used to ride all the way up to South Lake? I'd fish for the day and then coast back down."

"Really? From Bishop? Dude, that's insane."

"Gotta rely on rides now though, but it usually works out. Where you headed?" He held on to the handle above the passenger door while

Travis steered along the winding road through the short bluffs toward the reservoir.

"Meeting a friend up at Pine Creek for a hike. I'm takin' advantage of the last of summer before I start college."

"You're startin' college already?" He turned to look him over. Phantom didn't think Travis looked much bigger than when he first met him as a middle school kid. He stood straighter as if he was carrying more confidence, but he was still a skinny kid, wearing clothes that were more about utility than fashion and a dusty ball cap that did little to cover his unkempt brown hair.

"Yeah, I'm going to school in Utah to study art." He delivered the words with a nod as if still convincing himself of it.

"Art? I thought you wanted to be a research biologist or somethin'?" He'd told Phantom a year before he was pretty good at biology.

Travis smiled and shook his head, "Ya know, I always thought that's what I'd do. But I've really gotten into graphic design and photography. I had this awesome art teacher this year—he's actually an outdoor nut, too. You'd really like him—but he really got me excited about all this stuff."

Phantom offered a nod.

"Yeah, I've been hiking with my camera to some really great spots." His eyes widened, "Oh, dude, sometime I gotta show you these sweet shots I got up at Fossil Falls the other day. Man, if I can do that and get paid for it, sign me up."

"That's great to hear, bud. I wish I woulda had a teacher like that growing up. I never liked goin' to school 'cause the teachers were more like taskmasters." His eyes wandered just beyond the road toward Owens River, which sluggishly made its way south. "Learning was never fun, so I stopped going to school in eighth grade. Wasn't good at it anyway; never got above a C."

"Man, I would've never guessed that," Travis smiled and hit Phantom's arm with the back of his hand. "You're one of the smartest dudes I know."

"Well, experience is knowledge," Phantom turned his attention back to Travis. "I'd rather go taste or see or feel somethin' than read about it in a book. So, anyway, why'd you choose a school in Utah?"

"Yeah, ya know . . ." he smiled at Phantom a moment as if he was letting him in on a secret. "They have some great skiing and climbing up there."

"Oh yeah, I'll bet you're right." Phantom laughed, "And how's the school?" "Well, I don't know," he grinned. "I think it'll be good."

"Got your priorities, don't you?" Phantom returned the hit on his arm. "I'll be the last one to blame ya, though."

"So what've you been up to?" Travis asked as he blindly dug in his backpack behind his seat to pull out a water bottle covered in stickers. "I guess you don't have any tours today?"

"Well, I could if I wanted to," Phantom made sure to tell him. "With school out they're lining up, but I wanted to take a day off—" He paused a moment, realizing who he was saying all this to. He wondered if his dad, the game warden, still had it out for him. So he changed the subject. "Anyway, I put in a community garden in our apartment complex. That's going great. Everybody's chipping in to help. We already have cucumbers ready to be picked, and these aren't just any cucumbers." He stretched his hands more than two feet away from each other. "They've got to be the biggest in the state. Hoping to get some mammoth squash by the end of the season, too—"

"Hey, man, I want to tell you something," Travis interrupted. He suddenly looked as though he had something more important on his mind than college or vegetables. Phantom stopped mid-thought to look over at him. Travis just sat quiet for an uncomfortable amount of time as if he was thinking hard on something.

"So, what's on your mind, bud?"

He took a deep breath and let it out slowly. "I want you to know that I don't always see eye to eye with my dad."

"OK," Phantom offered.

"We got in an argument the other day about when he should put people away for breaking the rules up here and when he should just let things go." "Oh yeah," Phantom sat back in the seat waiting to hear where he was going with this. Travis' forehead was still wrinkled in either concentration or frustration. "So, are you saying I should keep things quiet for a while?" "Well . . ." he started, his answer lost in the breeze through his open window. "I respect my dad and what he does. He works his ass off." He took a sip from his water bottle. "You know he won Game Warden of the Year last year?"

"No, I didn't. Good for him," Phantom added, trying to nudge him to say what was really on his mind.

"It's tough to be a warden who actually enforces the law, especially in this area because everyone knows everyone, and they all talk. You know there are entire groups of people up here who don't like my family just 'cause my dad wrote up one of their buddies or relatives? No one wants someone showing up and ruining their fun, ya know? But he loves the beauty up here as much as anyone, and he's just trying to do his job—enforce the law and take care of this place."

"Yeah, I understand that," Phantom said, trying his best to keep his words to a minimum. "You don't want some punk kids coming up here and burning the whole place down."

"Yeah, exactly. I completely support what he's doing in a situation like that," he said, picking up steam now. "But I don't want him messing with what you're doing, just trying to share your experiences with people. He tells me it's not personal—it's not like he doesn't like you—he just doesn't like the way you're going about it. Thinks you're just full of tall tales. Aghh, I don't know," he hit his hand on the steering wheel in frustration. "I told him that you're helping preserve this place in your own way and he should just leave you alone." Before Phantom could respond, Travis shook his head and added, "Sorry, man."

Instead, Phantom smiled and asked, "So what changed your tune, Trav?" The wrinkles on his young forehead disappeared. He said gently, "Well, to be honest, I used to be sort of scared of you. This was before I really got to know you."

"What? Me? I weigh a whoppin' ninety pounds, bud."

"Well, maybe not scared. But I just didn't know what to think of you when you were always sitting out in front of Schat's. I was like fourteen, ya know, so all I knew is what people said about you. You know how folks are in Bishop these days. Anything too unusual must be a bad thing. Never mind that some of the oddest people up here— the real outdoor types—have been around this place the longest and make it worth sticking around."

He took a long sip from his stickered bottle as if it was fuel to keep him going, "Plus, when your dad's a law enforcement officer who comes home with stories of robberies and kidnappings, you grow up fearing strangers. He never liked me talking to random people, especially as a kid. And, ya know, at first you come off a bit . . . I don't know, strange."

Phantom blurted out a laugh. "Well, of course I do," he said, giving Travis permission to smile. "Life's too short to care what anyone thinks of ya."

"Yeah, for sure. And, ya know, I realized that a guy who spends most his time in front of the bakery, smiling and waving at people driving by, can't be a bad guy."

He brought the truck to a stop where the dirt road ended at a rusted metal gate. Beyond it, only a narrow footpath led to the reservoir. They both hopped out of the truck, their boots kicking up the valley's dust, a reminder that only a manmade body of water could survive there.

"Give me a hand, would ya?" Together they hoisted the bike from the truck bed.

"You want me to pick ya up on my way home?" he asked.

"Oh no. I'll ride back into town." Phantom put his cowboy hat in its place and swung his backpack over his shoulder. "Thanks for the ride up, though. And I'll do my best to stay outta trouble." He winked and tapped his hat with his finger as a thank you and started up the path.

"Hey, Phantom," Travis yelled after him a half a minute later. He stood in the driver's door of the pickup. "Don't worry about anything."

Phantom spun around, "What's that?"

"Keep doing what you're doing," he said.

Phantom smiled and didn't say anything at first. Instead, he looked down the path toward the young man who had a twinkle of excitement in his eyes for whatever he had planned that day. In that moment, Phantom spotted a glimmer of the old Bishop, and he wanted to tell Lauren all about it, right then and there.

"Thanks, bud," he yelled and tapped his hat with his finger. "I'll bring ya back a couple of big trout."

"Sounds like a deal." Travis ducked back into the truck and directed it east toward his own High Sierra adventure.

PHANTOM GOT A RIDE HOME later that day, but not the kind he'd wish on anybody.

He pulled his limit out of the reservoir, including a couple of big guys for Travis, and then decided to make a game of the last of a perfect Sierra day. He noticed the sun's spot in the sky, still a few fingers distance above Mount Tom, and he challenged himself to catch and release at least three more fish before the sun set.

"I'm racing the clock," he whispered to himself. "Let's go."

Just as he secured a fresh fly onto his line, he heard shouts and laughter coming up the path that leads to the reservoir. Two men and one woman appeared, carrying beer cans and a radio, and they made their way to a spot a few hundred feet from Phantom, who watched them with a scowl they didn't seem to notice. Between their chattering, they took turns casting until one of them got close enough to send a line, led by an impaled earthworm, flying over Phantom's line.

"Come on now!" Phantom cleared his throat so his voice would boom in their direction. This was the excuse he had been waiting for to set them straight. "Why don't you give me a little space here?"

The way Phantom told the story, one of the men yelled back, "Why don't we throw your ass in instead?"

"Keep talking, and I'll have you thrown out of this place for life," Phantom spit back.

"Really?" the woman started. "Under what authority?"

"My authority," he exaggerated. "This is more my mountain than yours; that's for damn sure."

At this point, the yelling had scared away even the hungriest fish, so Phantom figured he might as well call it quits. He cut his line, gathered his gear, and hiked past the fishermen's big Chevy truck to his bike to start his coast down 395, grumbling about the incident all the way down. Thirty minutes later, the mountaineer was just a dot amid the vast high desert, inching east along the highway under a dark navy sky. He breathed in the valley's cool evening air that somehow felt fresher and cleaner than what it had to offer in the daytime, and he kept his eyes on the lights of Bishop a few miles ahead.

He shook his head, half wishing his run-in with that group had happened at South Lake, where he could have pointed out the Anglers' Code of Conduct that's handwritten and nailed near the entrance of Parchers Resort. It was a list of unspoken rules, a gentle reminder to people who were going to fish in the water to treat the place with respect.

It read like this:

1. Don't cast near any other angler. With all the liquid on this mountain, there's no need to crowd along the water's edge.

2. Quickly release fish that you're not planning on holding on to. The longer they're out of the water, the higher risk of them dying.

3. Don't drag an eighteen-pack of Budweiser up here with you and leave behind a trail of empty beer cans and cigarette butts. This place is sacred.

4. On that note, don't leave a trace at all. Take every piece of wrapper, fishing line, and whatever else you brought back home with you.

5. Don't bring a radio. If you're tempted to break into a quiet humming rendition of 'Rocky Mountain High,' that's fine, but respect the peacefulness of the Sierras.

Phantom sighed and did his best to turn his thoughts toward what sort of projects he wanted to work on that night; he was behind on his fly-tying, and he needed to pick up a few groceries. Before he could finish his mental to-do list, he saw the empty space in front of him suddenly shine under two beams of yellow light. His fingers clenched the handlebars, and his whole frame braced, as if in an instinctive prayer, when he heard the rumble of eight cylinders. He swore he heard the sound grow to a loud roar, as though the driver had stomped on the gas pedal of a diesel truck, and then he felt a slam.

He crashed to the gravel, chest first, and rolled over desert brush until he finally came to a stop at the bottom of a ditch.

He didn't know how long he was unconscious, but when he awoke, everything was pitch black, and all he could feel was pain. Blood covered his hands and arms; his right shoulder and ribs throbbed. Lying there, he wished he didn't have to breathe, because every time his lungs sucked in air, it felt like he was irritating a fresh wound.

His eyes, burning from the blood that dripped down his face, were drawn to the only light, the stars, brighter out there than almost anywhere else. He probably passed out two or three more times, looking up at the twinkles with hope and then falling unconscious again, until he finally convinced himself to try to get help. He bit his lower lip in determination before slowly and painfully crawling toward the road, where he waited. He fought unconsciousness for an hour or more, uncontrollably shivering and grimacing with each breath. When the valley's blackness finally lit up under a pair of headlights, he stretched an arm toward the sky. A minivan whooshed by before coming to a stop a few seconds later.

He heard a slam of a car door and the crunch of gravel beneath heavy boots.

His arm fell. Everything went numb. All he could feel was the sting of the valley's dust in his eyes.

CHAPTER

Overcast

(v.) To cast a lure, fly or bait beyond the aimed-for target.

"I'M GONNA FIND THOSE GUYS." The words, meant as much a prayer as a promise, came out of Sierra Phantom with purpose as he laid broken on his thrift store couch.

"I hope you do, Phantom," Rennie offered in her soft, measured tone. She had come to his apartment to deliver a dish of chicken casserole, continuing her effort to make sure her friend had enough food, rest and company during this stretch of recovery.

The plunge into the ditch not only left Phantom with four broken ribs and torn rotator cuffs, but it also jarred the artificial tear duct and stent the doctors had put in after his first accident. This triggered his right eye to squirt tears without warning, so he had to return to UCLA to get everything resituated. This time, Rennie's son, Mark, drove him down to LA.

In the weeks that followed, Phantom targeted what little physical energy he had each day on assigned therapy exercises with the hope of fishing before the lakes froze over. Meanwhile, his thoughts were centered on bringing the person who hit him to justice.

"Now, don't be upset if you don't find these guys," Rennie continued. "They're probably from out of state somewhere and won't be easy to find." "Well, the deputy told me they're doing their part to try to get 'em.

If they don't, I've got eight thousand dollars worth of medical bills that I'm expected to pay. Plus, a pair of new glasses and my Huffy to replace," he said, pulling the last cigarette from a pack. "And, you know what, it's not even about that. These people should face some sort of punishment. It was drunk driving, a hit and run—attempted murder," he stressed that last accusation. "I can't handle knowing they're out there, scot-free."

Right then the phone rang, interrupting his rant. "Hello, Phantom here." "Mr. Glover . . ."

He held the phone away from him and whispered to Rennie, "Speak of the devil."

"We think we found the woman who hit you . . ." a sturdy-voiced deputy said, sounding as if he were reading from a script.

"Woman?"

"Yes, sir. She lives in San Diego . . ." He wouldn't say much about her, but he told Phantom to be in court at 9:00 a.m. on the ninth of October.

"Alrighty, I can do that. Thank you, deputy—Hey, can I bring you a couple Schat's pastries as a thank you? I'd bring ya fish, but I'm not supposed to be on the water for another month."

"No, sir. I'm just doing my job." "Alrighty, well, have a good day."

Rennie sat up straight in Phantom's creaky, thrift store chair and asked, "So what's the news?"

"We're goin' to court," he said with wide eyes, revealing a feeling of happy malice.

"Oh, really?"

"Oh," he said louder and more excitedly than he meant to, "and they're going to reimburse me for some new glasses and a new bike." He smiled, "How 'bout that?"

"Well, that's good news," she nodded and pressed her lips together in thought. "Hey, you want to get outta here?"

"You kidding me?" he said with raised eyebrows. "No, let's get out of this apartment for a few minutes."

Phantom stood up as if to make an important announcement and said, "Let's go to South Lake."

"Well, I don't know about that—I was thinking we could just grab a coffee and pastry. The doctors say you need a few more weeks before you start fishing again."

"But they don't know my strength. All they see is what's in some manila folder: I'm an old man who got hit by a car. I guarantee you I'll feel better—healthier—as soon as I'm breathing in that mountain air."

"You really think that's a good—"

"I think it's an excellent idea." He put his arms on his hips and flashed an exaggerated salesman grin.

Rennie pressed her lips together and looked at the colorless carpet in thought. Then she whispered as if the doctors were in the next room, "Well, as long as we take it easy." Phantom let out a loud laugh and lifted his cowboy hat from the coffee table to his head. "We really shouldn't miss out on a day at the lake," she added.

"Exactly! It's beautiful out."

She laughed along with him but then tried to sound like the more responsible one of the two. "Well, let me run home and pack us a lunch."

"Sounds like a swinging safari to me. I'll get my gear together." When she returned, Phantom was already standing outside wearing an eager grin and his backpack that was brimming with his usual fishing equipment. In each hand he held plastic grocery bags brimming with vegetables.

He set them in the truck bed and then gingerly pulled himself into the passenger's seat before doing his best to jerk the heavy door shut. Becky greeted him with a lick on his cheek. "Hey there, little lady," he said, scratching behind the corgi's pointed ears.

"So what'd you bring me?" Rennie asked.

"Oh, you're gonna love 'em," he said and went on about how well the community garden was going. "I'll get you a bunch of fish before the day's out, too."

"Well, now don't give all of your food away. Who knows how many fish you'll catch," Rennie added.

He paused for half a second and looked her direction. "Well, I usually catch at least a dozen more than the state limit."

"Oh, yes. I'm sure. Sorry, I didn't mean anything by that. I just—"

He continued, "I've pulled as many as seventy fish out of the water in one day. It's these glitter flies. I'm telling you, they're like magnets for these trout."

Rennie listened to him go on about his techniques as she rolled the window down to let the wind whip through the cab.

"That's the fresh air I've been cravin'," he said after a while, as he rolled down the passenger window. He breathed as deeply as his sore ribs would allow and enjoyed the welcoming scent of pine needles that was perpetually in the dry Sierra air.

"Sometimes I forget how lucky we are to live in such a pretty place," Rennie said, taking her eyes off the road just long enough to look up at the slick rock on either side of Highway 168. It was just a tease compared to the beauty that towered hundreds of feet above that. Within twenty minutes, they could see the aspen groves that lead to Mist Falls, a favorite place to spot the yellow and orange foliage each fall. Then Hurd Peak, dusted with snow for much of the year, and then the bumps of the Inconsolable Range.

The old pickup's grumble grew into more of a whine as the elevation approached ten thousand feet and carried Phantom and Rennie to the main entrance of Parchers Resort.

Phantom grabbed his gear and started toward the water while Rennie dug out her book and blanket and followed behind him. He avoided his usual spot, over the dam and beyond several feet of large rocks, because he knew it would be too difficult for Rennie to reach. Instead, he settled for fishing off the resort's dock.

He secured a fly on his line and got back to his favorite routine. It'd been almost two months since he had been on the water, and as he cast and reeled in and cast again, he felt as though he had come up for the only air he ever felt quite right inhaling. At moments he was busy tying flies or unhooking another trout, and other times he stared toward the peaks just beyond the water, stroking his beard as if he were taking in a familiar painting.

At one point Rennie asked with some hesitation, "How you doing without your cigarettes?"

"Oh fine. Don't need those things up here."

On their way back to town that evening, Phantom convinced Rennie to make a stop at Denny's. "That sounds good. I'm ready for dinner," she said as they approached Bishop. "I'll need to drop Becky off at home first."

"Well, I was actually just going to drop off fish for my servers, but yeah, let's get a bite to eat. I usually make all my deliveries on my bike, but if you've got time, I'll take the help."

"Sure, I don't have anywhere to be. Although, I'm eager to know if Dr.

Tori killed the senator," she said with big eyes and a thin smile. "What's that?"

As she turned into the Denny's parking lot, she laughed, "Oh, that's what's happening in this book I'm reading right now. The main character, Dr. Tori, I'm pretty sure she's the murderer." Phantom laughed along with her. "But I can wait to find out."

He led Rennie to his usual booth at the very back of the noisy restaurant. "Hola, Sierra Phantom!" He heard the familiar croon from Erica, who had emerged from the kitchen with plates of burgers and fries stacked along one arm. "You want your usual?"

"Yes, ma'am," he said, "but give my friend here a minute to look over the menu."

She smiled and pulled a menu from her apron and handed it to Rennie. "Take your time."

Phantom took off his cowboy hat and set it next to him in the booth. "I like sitting in her section," he said over the noise of banging dishes and orders yelled among the kitchen staff. He rested his arms on the back of the bench. "We sort of understand each other." Rennie smiled at him and continued to scan the menu. "You know, people aren't very kind to Mexicans in this town. They're some of the hardest working people I know, and you won't hear them complain about a thing."

She looked up from the menu and said softly, "I have noticed Bishop is more segregated than anyone wants to admit."

Without being asked, Erica delivered a cup of coffee for Phantom and then smiled at Rennie. "Alrighty, what can I get for you?"

"Hmm, I think I'll get your turkey burger and an iced tea."

"Sounds good." She turned to Phantom and asked, "Coffee and fries tonight?"

"Sounds perfect." He looked at Rennie with big eyes and added, "And how 'bout a strawberry shake?"

She nodded, "I won't turn that down."

"Good choice," Erica smiled. She disappeared into the kitchen, and Phantom gave Rennie a nod to encourage her to pick up where she left off.

"What were you sayin'?"

"Oh, it's just that . . . well, this town is sort of funny when you think about it. It's a place of contradictions as I see it."

"Contradictions?"

"Well, yes. All of its shops and restaurants and motels—the whole town, really—depends on the tourists who come through. But most of the people who've lived up here forever are as cranky as snakes about outsiders coming in."

"Yep, I hear ya there," he added.

"Take my son Mark. He's been dating this same sweet gal for a couple of years now, and her family still considers him an outsider because he's only lived up here—what is it now?—eight years. I guess they don't want people from LA moving here and ruining their peaceful town. But goodness, they don't have to be so stiff about it."

Erica delivered an iced tea and quickly moved on to serve other tables. Rennie continued, "Seems like everyone's slate of friends is full. They belong to the Elks Club, the VFW or the Lions Club, and then the young people have their little hang out at Rusty's. So if you're new, you have to make a real concerted effort to make friends."

Phantom nodded. "Ya know, when I moved down here, I was pretty upset with how much the character of the place had changed over fifty some years." He took a gulp of coffee. "I mean, I had seen it gradually changin'. I'd drop into town every few months. But living every day here made all those changes real."

Rennie nodded as she dumped a packet of Sweet'N Low into her tea. "Yeah, different crowd now," he nodded. "Hell, back then, it only drew one kind of person, and that was the tough-as-nails type. There was no Kmart. No Denny's. You couldn't rely on anything or anyone else to carry you. Surviving was up to you."

She took a sip of tea and sat back in the booth as though she was mulling over an idea. "See, I think it's still that way," she started slowly, as she usually did. "I think it just draws a different kind of survivor now: people who've braved their own storms. It draws people who didn't quite fit in LA, maybe 'cause it was too expensive, too cushy, or too crowded, which was the case for Mark and me." She paused half a second. "And it attracts people who found Las Vegas too flashy or Colorado too predictable. I don't think most of them could even quite say why, but for some reason they were drawn to this place, wedged between a desert on one side and mountains on the other."

Phantom smiled through his bushy beard because she was putting words to something he had never been able to before. He looked up at Rennie and added with a deep laugh, "And then there's us, huh?"

She joined him, "Well, don't get me started there."

"A flatlander and an old mountaineer sharing shakes and fries together." "I don't see the problem," she smiled. Then she offered one last thought on the couple of miles of civilization that surrounded them. "But you know, there is just something great about this place that you can't find anywhere else. I can't really pinpoint it." She took another sip of her tea. "It's like that quirky friend you don't quite understand, but you don't want to live without."

Phantom nodded and smiled as Erica arrived with dinner. "Here you go. Need anything else?" They shook their heads.

"Thank you, hon," he said.

After they talked awhile longer, Rennie caught a glimpse of the clock on the wall and blurted, "Phantom, it's almost nine. You sure you don't want to call it a night? You've really done a lot today. I almost forgot you were on the mend."

"What? I feel better than ever," he assured her, "and it's just a few stops." "I guess," she sighed and gave him a look. "If you feel up to it."

He left the biggest catch of the day for Erica because, as Phantom told Rennie, she had three kids and a bunch of nieces and nephews to feed. Next, he convinced Rennie to make a pit stop just a couple blocks west at the smoke shop at Paiute Palace Casino. Then, with her as his co-pilot, they made a few other drops around town. He directed her to a tiny, rundown house on the south end of town. "This is Maggie's place, from the thrift store," he said as he opened the truck door. He pulled a fish from the cooler and slid it into a plastic bag. When he returned, he added, "She's gettin' up there and lives by herself, so I like giving her fish. Next stop: Short Street."

He had her park in front of the row of rundown mobile homes that were tucked two blocks off Main Street, just across from Phantom's apartment complex. Not one streetlight on the small alleyway was lit.

"I never knew this little street was here," Rennie said, following his lead to park in front of a white mobile home that looked older than Phantom.

"She's a single mom with two kids," he explained to Rennie as he slid two fish into a plastic bag. He walked up the creaky steps and felt like he rattled the entire home with his knock. The oldest of the kids, a brown-haired boy in Teenage Mutant Ninja Turtles pajamas, opened the door.

"I've got something for ya, Daniel," Phantom smiled and held up the bag of fish.

Without saying a word, the boy ran away from the door and out of sight. After a couple minutes went by with no further sight of him, Phantom finally peeked his head into the trailer saying, "Daniel?"

When the boy finally emerged, he held a piece of gum high over his head and said, "Trade?"

"Deal." Phantom knelt and handed him the fish. He unwrapped the Doublemint and popped it in his mouth. "So, you been good? Keeping up with your homework and watching your little sister?"

"Mmm hmm," the boy stood up straight and nodded.

"Good man. Hey, I need to take you out on a fishing trip with me some time. Let's ask your mom if we can plan somethin' like that. It'd be a real adventure."

Daniel's eyebrows shot up, and he quickly nodded.

"OK, keep up your good work," Phantom said and offered a high five too high for him to reach without a good jump. The boy leapt up and laughed with the slap. "See ya, bud."

When Phantom climbed back into the truck, Rennie whispered, "He gave you gum?"

"He insisted," he smiled. "Sorry that took so long. The mom works the night shift, so I like to check in on the kids."

"That's OK. I have nothing to get to," she added, and she got the truck rolling toward his apartment. "I love seeing you in action, Phantom. I never knew you . . ." She paused and offered a quiet smile. Once the truck was in park in front of the apartment, she added, "You're like the Robin Hood of Bishop."

"Well, there's no need for fish to go to waste when there's someone who can use it." Phantom never thought much of his deliveries. He figured they'd do the same for him.

He brought the last of the fish to his neighbor Steven. He answered the door of Apartment 16 with a big grin. "Want to give that pan-fried trout another go?" Phantom asked.

"Yeah," he nodded and gave Phantom his usual slow high five.

They chatted a bit more until Phantom finally walked back to the truck. "Steve loves my trout," he said, out of breath, through the truck's passenger window. "Last week, I taught him how to fry it up in a pan, so he's really excited to try it on his own."

"He probably appreciates having a neighbor like you." Rennie sat back in the driver's seat and let out a slow exhale, as if she was taking a moment to appreciate a good day.

"See, I knew it'd be great to get out."

She laughed, "Yes, yes. You were right there. Get a good night's rest tonight, though."

He nodded in agreement and went to grab his fishing gear from the truck bed. "Oh no, Rennie," he said, looking up from his cooler, "I gave away my last fish. I meant to hold on to one for you."

"Oh, that's OK. I'm fine. Plus, I have all those veggies."

"Well, that's not enough for a meal," he said. "I think we'll just have to share some of that casserole tomorrow for dinner."

CHAPTER

Transition

(n.) A way of moving from one section of a story to another.

I'VE NEVER BEEN VERY GOOD at staying in one place for long. About the time Phantom and my weekly talks had gained momentum, I gave in to curiosity and took a new job. It turned out to be an occupational adventure I was not cut out for. It's a line on my résumé that reads like a hiccup: Legislative Correspondent, U.S. House of Representatives.

Within a week, I discovered I'd made the wrong choice. It was early mornings, lengthy subway rides, metal detectors, plastic grins and long marches along marble hallways in cheap high heels past impressive statues of people who I'm sure helped direct our nation's course in some profound way. But their bronze figures did little to convince me I could do anything world-changing in this job.

Twice a week, I stayed at a friend's apartment in the city to take a break from the long commute. After work, I'd jog along the National Mall, return to the apartment, microwave a frozen dinner and, like clockwork, call Sierra Phantom.

On those nights, our conversations became about more than just chronicling an old man's story. They became an escape from this place that seemed more concerned about the appearance of doing good work rather than actually doing it. I missed a cluttered newsroom and journalists who got paid half as much as my new coworkers for the pure satisfaction that they were improving their little corner of the world. I missed good stories. But as soon as I heard, "Hellooo, Phantom here," my shoulders— tense from the bus, the train, the suits, the disguise—relaxed. His voice came through the phone strong and assured but friendly. He never asked much about me, which was fine. This was about him. But even when he was talking about his recovery since his accident, his prized cucumbers, or his new fishing buddy, it was his voice that made me feel safe and encouraged and free right along with him.

"I've started getting some of my strength back since my run-in with that truck," he started our conversation with one night. "My friend Rennie started driving me up to South Lake on occasion to get me back on the water. She doesn't fish, but she calls herself my fishing caddie. And for the last couple months I've been fishing with a guy named Ed. I met him up at the reservoir one afternoon after a long day of fishing." He delivered each sentence faster than the one before. I leaned back on the couch, with a reporter's notebook on my lap, and listened. "He'd heard about the hit and run and was just as mad as I was about it. So he told me, 'I don't care if it's two o'clock in the morning, we'll go fishing. You just call me.' He's a Navy 'Nam vet, so we get along real well. We're enjoying these little competitions. Whoever comes up short on fish has to clean the other guy's catch."

"Wait a second," I interrupted, "Mr. Phantom, I've never heard about how you got involved in the Navy." I looked down at a timeline of Phantom's life I'd scribbled in blue pen on my notebook to keep his story straight. "Was that after you lived in Chinatown?"

"Mmm hmm," he offered. "Yes, hon, I went straight from working for Hickman into the Navy."

"OK, wait a minute." I sat up and dug in my bag for my laptop. "Can you take us back there?"

"Well," he paused a second. "I s'pose . . ." I pulled up a blank page. "Let's see now . . ." he started again slowly and guided us back to Seattle, 1942. "I liked working for Hickman, but I've never been very good at staying in one place for long. I've always wanted to discover what's over that next mountain, through that forest or beyond that valley. So when I heard on the radio that the government was looking for volunteers to join the military, I was all ears."

"Really? Wasn't there a draft?"

"Well yeah. They couldn't get enough boys to volunteer. At that point I didn't really see it as entering a war, but as a ticket to see the world." He paused, and I heard the click of his lighter. "That memory is crystal clear. I was working in Hickman's workshop, and the radio, covered in sawdust, was blarin': 'We have a call for our nation's boys. Want to see the world, protect our nation, and get training for a career? Join one of the branches of the United States Armed Forces. This call is from the top, boys. Uncle Sam wants you!'

"I looked up at Hickman from whatever project I was working on. 'You hear that, Hickman? Uncle Sam wants you. You want to see the world?'

"'Kid, I'm too old for that stuff. Anyway, I've already seen it. What, you wanna see the world?'

"I paused a few seconds to think it over. 'Well, yeah. I do.' "'Well I guess you'll have to wait. You gotta be eighteen.'

"I went back to my work and just sorta mulled the idea over for the next few days. My sixteenth birthday was just around the corner, and I wasn't waitin' two more years to enlist.

"About a week later, I asked Hickman sorta out of the blue, 'What if you sneak me in?'

"'Huh? In where?'

"'The U.S. Navy.'"

Phantom laughed through the phone. "I don't know how I got these ideas in my head. I finally convinced him of what I wholeheartedly believed, and still believe to be true. With the knowledge I had, my country needed me.

"Hickman wrote a letter to the recruiting office, telling them I had been passed around from orphanage to orphanage, so I didn't have a birth certificate but that he could vouch for my age. They believed him, and a month later I boarded a bus for San Diego, where I'd join 180 other boys in my unit for basic training. As soon as I took my seat, I felt a surge of excitement. I was setting out to discover the world.

"When our unit arrived, we were all put in quarantine for six weeks. We spent most of the time in hospital robes, getting poked and prodded by doctors, making sure our health could handle what war would surely throw at us. They sent all 180 of us through a makeshift barber shop in just two days. Those barbers ran a swift operation. They had each guy's head shaved before he could even get comfy in the chair.

"When it was finally my turn in the chair I joked with the barber, 'Mmm, I'll just take a trim. Go ahead and leave the sideburns.'"

"That was gutsy. Did he shave you bald?" I asked with a laugh.

"I'll be damned if the barber didn't give me exactly what I asked for. I didn't ask why he let me get away with it, but I walked out laughing at the whole thing. Well, the next day I saw Vice Admiral McMorris in the mess hall—he was the commander of the Pacific Fleet Frontier. 'Nice sideburns,' he said to me while I was in line for dinner.

"'Thank you, sir,' I said, ya know, waiting for my scolding.

"He told me it was him who gave the barber the OK to keep my hair however I wanted it. 'Of all these guys, you're the only one who wants to be here. We appreciate your willingness to jump in and serve your country.'

"Not only was I the only volunteer, but I was also the youngest, and I came in with more knowledge on how to stay alive in tough circumstances than all the other guys combined."

He paused a second. So I asked, "What do you mean?"

"Everything I had experienced throughout my life prepared me for the Navy. When your life is dependent on split-second decisions, you become flexible in a way that you have complete contentment in any situation you're in. You have to prepare for the worst and know how to make do under as many possible conditions as you can imagine. When it comes to survival, it's as if it was ingrained in me.

"Another thing I realized was how tough most of the kids I grew up with were . . . at least compared to some of these Navy guys. A lot of them were mama's boys who had never stepped out of their comfort zones. They didn't even know how to wash their own socks. While that meant I had to teach them some basic life skills, it also made it even easier to get noticed by my officers.

"I was the star student. Like in a sailing class, the officer would ask, 'What's port? How about starboard?' With each question, I shot up my hand. Because I worked on sailboats for some of the wealthier folks at the orphanage in Washington, I knew all these things, and nobody else could answer them. I even led the unit in the swim tests—I had a blast with those. The officers also discovered I had a keen eye for shooting."

He paused a moment. I imagined he was probably smoking. Then he added, "Seems like I'd been practicing for that all my life. I remember makin' my own slingshot out of rubber bands when I was about five years old. I had a pretty good eye for a little kid. I'd gather small stones and aim for tree branches and leaves. Then I'd move on to tougher targets. At one point, I tied a string around a dime and hung it from a tree. Then I'd walk 25 paces from the tree and shoot at the dime. When that became a cinch, I tapped the dime to send it swinging. Then, I'd step back and take aim at the pendulum. When I mastered that, I aimed for the string. By the time I was eight or nine, I could take the head off a flying mallard."

He stopped just long enough to catch his breath. Then continued at a rambling pace, "So, they had a choice to either put me on the Underwater Demolition Team, which was a newly formed elite combat group of swimmers, or to put me with the guys on shore. They decided to make me a sharpshooter and instructed me to study the terrain of Alaska as much as I could over the next several weeks. My job became, really, to keep the men alive.

"'We're sending you boys to the Aleutian Islands,' an officer finally told me.

"I couldn't believe my luck. I'd been interested in Alaska ever since I was a kid. I remember stepping off the plane and just stopping in my tracks to take it all in. It was like nothing I'd ever seen before."

"But it didn't take long for the mystique of it all to fade and be faced with why I was really there. The Army had gone into Alaska before us to fight thousands of Japs who had come over with a plan to build a base there and eventually gain control of the land. Most of those guys went in unprepared, maybe not for battle, but for the dangers of Alaska. The Army didn't give them a stick of warm clothing, so they'd come in with frostbite on their ears and toes," his tone hardened, still feeling that frustration. "More men died from not having the right supplies and knowhow than died in battle. It was awful.

"So the Navy officers warned us to be smart and learn from the mistakes of the units before us. They made me the number one sniper and asked me to help lead a survival school for the other boys. It wasn't easy for airplanes to get to us, so we had to provide a lot of the food ourselves, so I taught the guys how to hunt, fish, and find herbs and berries they could safely eat. I can honestly say that if it wasn't for me, they would'a lost a lot of men. It may sound prideful, but it's the truth . . ." I nodded and did my best to just listen.

"By the time we got our bearings, we learned that the Japanese had bombers loaded up on carriers ready to attack Seattle. The Japs sent out nine mountaineers to forecast the weather and tell the bombers when it was safe to take off. As soon as the Navy figured all this out, they sent me and a few others up there to send those guys incorrect codes to guide them into bad weather.

"In the summer of 1942, the Japs' bombers took off to attack Dutch Harbor on Unalaska Island before they knew a storm was headed their way. Only about half of the planes found the target, all because of our handiwork. Still, they did some damage. About 20 of their planes from two aircraft carriers dropped bombs on the base. They targeted the radio station and petroleum storage tanks. That was just six months after Pearl Harbor. You ever heard about any of this?"

"No," I said, caught off guard, before bashfully adding, "I mean, I'm not a history buff. Honestly, I didn't realize there were any troops in Alaska during World War II."

"Well, most people don't realize it," he said, making me feel better. "The Navy kept all this conflict in Alaska pretty quiet because they didn't want the nation panicking." He took a long pull from his cigarette. "Another day, we were out checking around the islands for German-Japanese subs that were trying to come in and unload food and arms caches. In fact, we were going diagonal to a German sub and we gave them three warnings to give up and they wouldn't do it. So the captain said 'ram them!' We cut 'em in half and didn't bother picking up any survivors."

"Oh my goodness," I said without meaning to.

He sighed, "Ya know, hon, I spent all four of my years in the Navy up there, and I hated it. I was a teenager doin' and seein' all this."

I carefully added, "Did you ever regret enlisting?"

"Well, I was never keen on fighting in the war. It was about seeing the world." Then he changed the subject, "I tried to keep my focus on the beauty of the place just to keep from going crazy. Whenever I could, I'd go out to explore the islands. It's beautiful up there."

"Mr. Phantom, will you talk about . . ." I started, gently, still nervous the wrong question could end what we'd spent all this time building. "What were your feelings about the fighting?"

He didn't say anything for several seconds. I held my breath to stop myself from saying any more. Then he said softly, "I saw horrible things that I really don't like to talk about." I almost took my question back, to let him off the hook, but he continued. "I had to shut my mind off to it. I had to think of it more or less like a game. We heard so many stories about the Japs torturing our troops, so we had no qualms about who was goin' to fire the first shot. I'll confess to ya now, I didn't even see them as human beings. It became no different than killing a deer. I gotta say, I really don't like to talk about all I saw up there," he said again. "In fact, I don't let anyone up here even question me about the war because a lot of things went on. I still have flashbacks about what happened up there to my buddies and everything. I was just ready to get out of there."

He paused long enough to take another pull on his cigarette, and I fought the temptation to add some useless line to usher in a more comfortable moment.

"I guess, yeah, I do regret it," he said, rushing the admission. "I actually thought I'd get back to Alaska one day, but something in me couldn't go back again. It probably would've been even harder to leave behind those memories." He stopped.

I started, "So, instead you…"

"So I headed to the Sierra Nevadas. And here I am." He took a deep breath and let it out slowly. Then added quietly, "There's a decision I never regretted."

CHAPTER

Back-wash

(n.) Rough water resulting from boat wakes rebounding off fixed objects, such as rocks.

———

SIERRA PHANTOM HAD NEVER been more eager to tell his story. It had started to feel like an addiction. He'd go a few moments each day without thinking about it, but then pick it up again, running over and over through what he'd say to the judge if he got a moment to really let it fly. He was like an athlete preparing for competition, going through every possible question, and preparing his mind to retrieve any detail the court requested. He was ready.

But October 9 came and went without any hearing and without him "gettin' to see the whites of that woman's eyes," as he put it. He and Rennie drove to Independence and spent two hours warming the hard pews of the Inyo County Courthouse before they were told the woman suspected of hitting Phantom would not be there. She had a conflict.

The judge postponed the hearing, so a month later, Rennie and Phantom piled into the truck and headed toward Independence to try it again. Phantom's new fishing buddy Ed tagged along for support. "Would you recognize her if you saw her?" Ed asked as they started the forty-mile drive south.

"Think so. I'd sure as hell recognize the two men she was with," his eyes burned just thinking about them. "They were fishing like maniacs, acting like they owned the place."

Rennie and Ed got to talking about where they grew up and how they ended up in Bishop. Phantom looked out the window, and returned to the thought that had held him captive for months.

". . . You know, I worked hard all my life so I could just go fishing anytime I wanted. And here I am," Ed went on to Rennie. "I try to keep it to three days a week. Now, Phantom on the other hand, would fish every day of his life if he could, right man?" He hit Phantom's arm with his hand to nudge him to join the conversation.

"Yes, sir," Phantom offered, but he kept his gaze out the window. "I'm telling you, I'm glad I met this guy," Ed said. "Phantom and me are sort of kindred spirits."

His friend offered a gentle nod, "A good team."

"We both love fishing," Ed continued. "And we're both war vets. Different wars, of course. But, ya know . . ."

They sat quiet a minute; the beige scenery framed in the car windows giving them nothing to look at or comment on, no excuse to change the subject. Rennie, who was performing her usual balancing act with her coffee between her knees, lifted the travel mug to take a sip. Then, as if she had decided to ask an important question and wanted to deliver it before she'd lost the courage, she blurted out quickly, "Were you in Vietnam?"

Ed looked at her a second in the rearview mirror before he nodded and dug into the bag of Schat's pastries Rennie had picked up. And they were all quiet again. Phantom was the only one who noticed the fuzzy lyrics through the Ford's shoddy speakers: "Stop, hey, what's that sound. Everybody look what's going down . . ."

A half-minute later, Rennie broke the silence by saying, "You know, my husband was a war vet?"

Ed politely nodded. Phantom sat up straight and turned toward her. "Rennie, you were married?"

"I was," she half-smiled. He kept his eyes on her and waited for her to offer more. "Yes, I met him right after high school. Believe it or not, he was twenty-one years older than me."

"Twenty-one years?" Ed said.

"You know, when you're eighteen and a handsome military man in his late thirties asks you out, you're not gonna turn him down. And he was handsome," she stressed the words with a smile.

They laughed, and Ed added, "Girls like their men in uniforms."

"So . . ." Phantom started slowly, "what happened to him?"

"Well, he was never quite the same after the war." She pulled in a breath and let it out slowly. She pressed her lips together as if to keep the answer from escaping, and then only offered, "We were married 12 years before he passed away."

The two men sat quiet; their eyes directed out the window, where homes started to appear as the truck delivered them into the town limits of Independence. Rennie felt the need to end the drive on a more positive note, so she added, "You know, one small good came of it. Because his death was considered a consequence of the war, I got to go to college on his G.I. Bill. And that's how I got into teaching. I had to wait thirteen years after high school to go to college because my parents couldn't afford it. But, oh my word, when I got to be back in a classroom I was never so happy."

At that, the truck coasted to a stop in front of the huge, white courthouse of Inyo County. The appearance of the place hushed all three of them, as it does almost anyone coming from the county's smallest towns. By the look of it, county leaders wanted to ensure that anyone who wasn't already intimidated to go to court would be before they set foot on its steps.

Four three-story-tall pillars greeted guests, if that's what you'd call them, and inside dark, heavy oak made up the trim, doors, and casings, contrasted by cold marble floors that guaranteed attorneys would be able to hear each click of their fancy shoes on their way to court. "Looks like three-fourths of the county's taxes go to supporting the place," Phantom had thought when he had first seen the courthouse the month before. A sign just inside the entrance indicated that the building was built as the region's only example of "monumental neoclassical revival public architecture," whatever that meant.

"I never like walking into this place," Phantom whispered to Rennie and Ed on their way in.

"Well," Rennie added, "It certainly sticks out like the sore thumb of Inyo County."

The only expense county leaders spared on the building was a public elevator. So the three found the stairs and slowly made their way to the third floor. As she did four weeks earlier, Rennie gingerly hoisted herself up two flights of stairs with the help of her cane, and Phantom, whose ribs and shoulders still ached, didn't move much faster. By the time they had climbed to the courtroom, a colossal clock displayed behind the judge's bench let them know they were twelve minutes late.

They took a seat in the back of the room in the same miserable pews that weeks earlier Phantom had decided would cure most convicts from ever doing any wrong again. While they caught their breath, they watched the judge address a few small cases, like traffic violations and possession of marijuana.

"Listen, kid. Looks like you don't have much respect for the law," a black, heavyset judge said, looking down at a teenage boy from his elevated bench. "You've been caught stealing twice, and now you've been caught with marijuana. I'm giving you a five hundred dollar fine, and this time, you're spending time behind bars. Two months." The sternfaced young man was greeted by two officers and a pair of handcuffs.

Rennie looked at Phantom with wide eyes, and Ed quietly smirked, "I hope he's this tough on every offender."

Rennie whispered in Phantom's ear, "Is she here?"

He sat up straight to look down each of the pews for any familiar faces. He shook his head.

"I'll make sure we didn't miss it," Ed said. He walked to the back of the courtroom to talk to a bailiff, a tall, skinny man with posture that made him appear even taller. When Ed returned, he mumbled, "Come out in the hallway."

Phantom shook his head, looked at the judge, and then looked back at Ed. The way his luck was going, he thought the judge would start on his case the moment he stepped out.

Ed looked at him and added, "Trust me."

As the judge scolded a woman for a slew of unpaid speeding tickets, Rennie and Phantom stood as quietly as they could and hobbled out of the courtroom. They spotted Ed and the bailiff standing down the hallway another hundred yards away, so they made their way to them. Getting frustrated now, Phantom asked a little too loudly, "What's going on?"

"Did we miss the hearing?" Rennie asked breathlessly.

"We didn't miss it," Ed offered, and he looked toward the bailiff. "But it sounds like it may not happen."

"What in the hell?" Phantom responded, too loudly.

"Mr. Glover," the bailiff said softly, "you can't say you got this from me." He hunched slightly so he didn't have to raise his voice above a whisper. "The judge is throwing out the case."

"What?" Rennie and Phantom asked in unison.

"He doesn't think there's much of a case," he continued. "Much of a case?" Phantom asked.

"Well, apparently . . ." he started and stopped. He offered an uncomfortable smile and a "Morning" to two suited men who rushed past, one rolling a briefcase of files behind him as if he were walking a dog. The bailiff hunched lower. "Apparently," he started again, so quietly that Phantom had to step closer to hear him, so close that had anyone turned to look, they would've known a secret was being shared. "The woman who hit you is a deputy sheriff in some Southern California county—" His eyes looked hard at Phantom as though he wanted to say more, but he stopped. "You can't say where you got this information."

Phantom leaned back on his heels as if some force was trying to blow him over. "That's why they're throwin' this case out?" he whispered to himself through clenched teeth. "Is that what this is?" he added louder, directing the question toward the bailiff. Then he gave up on whispering, "So these deputies can uphold the law when it suits them, but they're protected from it themselves, huh?" He was now waving his hat around with each word. "They're goin' to let these people get away with this? It was drunk driving, a hit and run—attempted murder. God damned government."

"Sir, sir," the bailiff said softly, trying to not draw any more attention. His brown eyes looked straight at Phantom's until the old man finally nodded in agreement. "I gotta tell ya, sounds like she put all of her assets—her house, her car, everything—in her husband's name. So there's nothing to go after at this point."

Phantom clenched his teeth to stop himself from shouting. Rennie asked, "Well, can we do anything then?"

"Unfortunately, I really don't think so," he replied. "I'm sorry, Mr. Glover."

Without saying anything more, the bailiff led them to a nearby door. Hidden behind it was an elevator, saved only for court employees and the occasional prisoner. The four stepped inside, and the bailiff took a card from his pocket and waved it in front of a sensor before he hit the ground floor button.

"Thanks for letting us know all of this, sir," Rennie offered.

He nodded. Then, he looked down at Phantom and said, "Sorry again for how it turned out."

Phantom shook his head, but couldn't shake his scowl. As the elevator descended, the old man gulped in the overheated courthouse air and forced out the words, "It's not you I'm mad at." When the elevator door opened, he sucked in another deep breath and added with a heavy sigh, "You're just deliverin' the message."

CHAPTER

Keeper

(n.) For anglers, it is a fish worth taking home.

IN THE LONG DAYS THAT FOLLOWED the accident, Phantom spent more time at the doctor's office and in Apartment 14 than on the water. His physical therapist told him he should be patient with his recovery because he probably should've died right there in the gravel along 395, less than a mile from where he had built his first shelter decades earlier.

"Well, I'm a survivor . . . always have been," he told her bluntly.

She suggested her most stubborn patient wait until the next year's fishing season opened before he attempted any of his high elevation adventures. But that's like telling a trout to avoid water. By the time November came, Phantom was getting nervous he wouldn't get another chance to throw his line in one of the higher elevation lakes before the snow fell. So one day he woke up before dawn, packed his fishing gear, and pedaled over to Rennie's.

As soon as he turned the bike into her trailer park, he let it out with a wail, "Rennieee, you ready for an adventuurree?" He held each word for an extra second like they were being sung. With his fishing rod over his shoulder and his pack strapped to his back, he coasted past a half dozen trailer homes leading up to Rennie's. She had told him once that hers was the pale pink trailer at the end of all the white ones. As he pulled in front of it, he spotted Rennie peeking out one of its small windows, before she threw the shades shut. He brought the bike to a stop, put down the kickstand, and stood with arms crossed. "Rennieee? . . . The door cracked open to barely reveal his friend in a nightgown.

"You're up!" he exclaimed just as Becky squeezed past Rennie to greet him.

"Phantom," she whispered groggily. "What are you doing?"

"I have quite the day planned for us." He took off his cowboy hat for dramatic effect. "I'm thinking . . . a trip up to Lake Convict, enjoy the sunshine, catch a few fish. I already have lunch packed. What do ya say?" She sighed, "Oh, I don't know. Who knows what time I stayed up 'til last night." He kept his smile and his stance steady while she thought a few seconds and finally surrendered, "OK, OK, I'll go."

An hour later they were doing what they both enjoyed most, taking in the kind of beauty only offered at eight thousand feet above sea level. Phantom decided to take his friend to Convict Lake, about forty miles from Bishop. It had the closest thing to a beach that a mountain lake can offer, and he thought it would be the perfect spot for Rennie to throw down a blanket and read.

In the summer, it was always busy with tourists who wanted to see for themselves the place where a group of convicts hid out in the late 1800s after they'd escaped from a Carson City prison. The sheriff eventually caught up with them, but their escape left a big enough impression that someone decided to name the lake after them. Made for a good story. But Phantom liked to take people there for the fishing and the dramatic mountains that towered over its shores.

IT MIGHT HAVE BEEN the excitement of his first official outdoor road trip in weeks, but on this day the sun seemed to shine a bit brighter, the air felt cleaner, and the view was even more beautiful than he remembered. For the moment, he felt like he could forget about the woman who hit him. His focus was on the good that surrounded him, the here and now.

After a good few hours of casting, Phantom heard Rennie yell from the shore, "Ready for lunch?" He walked back to her with a string of fish and raised them to eye level with a showy grin. She giggled, "Is that what you meant when you said you'll provide lunch?"

"Now you know you love trout. . ." he joked, and he set the fish on a nearby rock. "Actually, I brought my usual lunch." Rennie knew that meant pancakes glued together with peanut butter. She thought they were so dry that a person could choke before they successfully swallowed them, but Phantom saw them as an easy source of protein.

"Sounds great," Rennie politely lied.

"Man, the fish are biting," he said, plopping down on the blanket. He set a bandana lined with pancakes between the two of them and waited for

Rennie to grab the first one. "They know winter's coming, so they're gettin' their fill now." He took a bite and noticed her book turned down on the blanket to mark her page. "What sort of drama you reading about now?"

"Oh, you might actually like this one. It's a mystery set in World War II. They think this American soldier is actually a spy for the Germans. The storyline is all twisted up, so I can't tell the good guys from the bad guys," she laughed, as she stretched out on the blanket. "It's great."

She nibbled for a minute before saying, "Hey, Phantom, can I ask you something?"

"Of course, hon," he said and held his breath.

"Reading this book got me thinking. . . what did you do after the war? Is that when you moved up here?"

"Well, sort of," he exhaled and did his best to hide the fact he'd stopped breathing for half a second. "Ya know, I thought I might stay in Alaska, just 'cause it was so wild and beautiful. I looked into buying a launch boat and starting a guide business, takin' people up and down from Alaska to British Columbia. But those launch boats are really expensive. So instead, I decided to get back to California. My lieutenant commander told me, for all I'd done for my unit, the Navy would send me wherever I wanted to go."

"Really? Well, that's nice. Anywhere in the world?"

He took a bite from an apple and said with a full mouth, "Yeah, I guess so. And ya know what I told 'em? I said, 'Ya know, I've always wanted to check out the Sierra Nevada Mountains.'"

"So you got your wish, and here you are?" Rennie asked matter-of-factly. "Yep, that's right," he said, providing the easier answer to that question. "I can't ever imagine you not living up here," she smiled. "It's like you're a part of the landscape or something. . ."

He nodded and offered a polite smile to indicate he was listening, which he wasn't. His fingers played with the blanket's fringe as he thought over whether to offer more. He looked up at her as though he was confessing some great sin and said, "Actually, that's not the full story."

"What do you mean?"

"I couldn't come up here right after the war," he added. "I was itchin'
to get up here to discover the place, but it was more than a year before I
made it." His fingers made their way to his shirt pocket, subconsciously
searching for his pack of smokes, which he'd left at the apartment. They
settled for the fringe on the blanket. "First I had to spend six months at a
base waiting for my discharge. They sent me to the Navy base on Treasure
Island. You ever been there?"

"Hmm. . ." she thought. "Is that the little island that you see when you
cross the Bay Bridge to San Francisco?"

He nodded.

"I've seen the sign for the exit." She said with bright eyes and a smile to
match, "It sounds kind of magical, Treasure Island."

"Yeah, s'pose it does," he laughed a little. "But it's nothing like it
sounds. It's just a big slab of concrete. Just a square mile of parking lots
and dormitories. But, the Navy gave me a lot of flexibility while I was
there. They'd let me take the bus into San Francisco, hang out in Golden
Gate Park. I ate my way through Chinatown, and I didn't have to do night
watches."

He paused a few seconds, long enough to think over how much he
wanted to go into. His fingers kept twirling bits of the blanket; his gaze
stayed on his hands without meaning to. "She's not asking for anything,"
he thought, "she just wants to know me." So he kept talking, "But they
assigned me to funeral detail, which I'd say was worse than any night watch.
Our team buried soldiers, and my job as a squad leader was to warn the
family of the gunshots fired during each funeral service. And even though I
knew they were comin', each fired shot shook me to my core. It really was
all nerve wracking. You know, these families were going through such a
tragedy and just trying to get this day behind them . . ."

He took a long drink from his water bottle and continued, "One
morning a gal jumped on to her son's casket. It took six of us guys to pull

her off." He looked up at Rennie. Her eyes were less bright now, her lips pressed together as if she was stopping herself from speaking or maybe tearing up. "It's tough to just forget those kinds of scenes." He shook his head as if to rid his mind of the memory and turned his stare to the other side of the lake. "For a lot of these guys, returning from war was a battle in itself. We were bitter after what we saw: the fighting, the torture, buddies dying left and right."

His eyes looked back to her, and in a stern whisper he said, "We learned to hate our fellow man. You'd think home would bring comfort, but for so many of 'em, they couldn't just snap back into some peachy-keen life. And I never even had a life like that to begin with. A lot of the guys couldn't find jobs when they came back because so many women had filled the positions while the men were off at war. Some ended up committing suicide because they didn't know what else to do with themselves. All of it became too much for me to sit back and watch. I was ready to get the hell out of there. I thought, 'You know if society wants to go and blow themselves up, let them do it. Just leave me out of it.'

"At base, I'd daydream about my plans after the Navy," he said, softening his tone. "I started seriously thinking about the ins and outs of preparing to live in the mountains. I knew enough not to just take off without learning about the terrain, the weather patterns, the food supply, and all that. So as soon as I got my discharge letter, I set out to find a job." He started on his apple again. "Like I said, jobs were hard to come by, so I really had to charm someone to get hired. Mr. Hickman, the carpenter I worked for as an apprentice before the war, always told me to be a jack-of-all-trades, so I'd never be out of a job and never go hungry. He also told me to know how to sell myself. 'Be so damn good that they can't afford not to hire you,' he'd tell me. That's exactly what I was thinking when I walked into a Walgreens in San Francisco. And, oh Rennie, did I work my magic. I sounded like a real salesman."

She smiled, "That doesn't surprise me one bit."

"I walked right up to an older man standing behind the cash register and said, 'Sir, I have an opportunity for you. I can help you with maintenance and stocking shelves. I'm great with people. I'm really a jack-of-all-trades, just coming back from fighting in Alaska with the Navy. I'm the best employee you'll ever hire. You got any openings?' Then I flashed him a big grin. He stepped back a minute as if he was weighing whether I was a nut, which that city was already known for, or a smart kid with true grit. He finally said, 'Well, I guess I could use some help around here,' and right on the spot he offered me a job as assistant manager."

"Wow, assistant manager?"

He nodded and took one last bite of his apple. "It was a pretty good job, too. You know, I wasn't working with my hands, but I've always been good with people, so I liked that part of it. I also got a job washing windows, so I could pull in $3,000 a month easy. I wanted to save up as much money as I could while getting ready to leave. And when I wasn't on the clock, I was preparing."

"Preparing?" Rennie asked.

"Well, mostly I built up a food supply. I stashed away dried eggs, dried milk, macaroni, rice, oatmeal, candy bars, and cigarettes in boxes about this big," he gestured with his hands. "I'd get each paycheck cashed into one hundred dollar bills, and in each food box I taped one or two bills. All together I had about 35 boxes, and my friend agreed to ship me them as I needed them. Then I found mountain guides who could tell me about the weather patterns. You ever thought about how much snow Mammoth gets compared to everything around it?"

She smiled and nodded, "No, not really."

"I researched all this before I got up here. I found out that the range between Big Pine all the way to Mammoth runs about fourteen thousand feet on average. Mammoth Mountain creates a nook at eleven thousand feet on that side of the range, so it catches most of the snow while everything on the other side, South Lake, Bishop, and all that, is much more protected.

That's why I decided to set up my camps on that side of the mountain, starting at South Lake. So when I had all that figured out and had enough money saved up, I took a Greyhound bus from San Francisco to Visalia. Then, I hitched rides as far up the mountain as I could and gradually made my way up to South Lake. And there ya have it."

Rennie laughed at his abrupt stop. "I love hearing all this, Phantom. I think it's amazing how you've lived."

He gave a wordless smile before standing up to stretch. "Think I might hit the water again, try to snag a couple more big guys." He grabbed his rod, started toward the shore, and yelled over his shoulder, "Cross your fingers for a golden trout."

While his boots carried him halfway around the lake to test his glitter flies out in another spot, his thoughts kept nudging him to appreciate a day in the fresh air with good company. He closed his eyes and turned his face south to be warmed by the autumn sun; then he slowly inhaled the chilly oxygen. He exhaled and opened his eyes to get back to the fish, but his eyes caught Rennie, sitting on her blanket with her nose in that book. She must've sensed his glance because she looked up and gave a smile and a little wave. He smiled back and offered his own wave. Then he got to casting.

When the sun finally started to drop, he caught and released his last trout and made his way back over to Rennie, who was throwing Becky a stick. When the corgi saw him coming with a string of fish, she forgot all about the lifeless twig and bolted his direction.

"Sorry, Becky, you're not gettin' any of these guys." "Ready to call it a day?" Rennie asked.

"Yes, ma'am. I think I've caught and released every fish in Convict Lake." "Looks like you got some good ones," she offered and threw one last stick for Becky. "She's not very good at fetch," she said with a laugh as she watched the dog sprint toward the stick, give it a sniff, and then hurry back for another.

"She must think it's an exercise for you," Phantom laughed, before carefully packing his tackle in his backpack. "Feels good to get out of the house and stand in the sunshine," he said, more to himself than to Rennie, and then he hoisted the pack and his rod in to the truck bed.

"I'm glad we came," she added.

Phantom leaned against the truck and took another deep, satisfying breath as he looked out over the water. It looked as though he was just taking a final glance at the lake, but he was deep in thought. He was mulling over an idea that had been on his mind for weeks now, and he was pushing himself to share it.

"Come on, Becky," Rennie yelled and slapped her thigh to get the dog's attention. She picked up the pup, with its squatty legs, and helped her climb into the driver's seat of the truck. "In you go."

Phantom's eyes turned from the water to his friend. "Ya know, hon . . ." he started but stopped.

"Yes," she asked nonchalantly as she pulled her keys from her purse. He took a deep breath and then delivered the next words too quickly. "I gotta tell ya, I'm not the marrying kind, but if I ever had been, you woulda been the girl for me." He gave one short nod, content that he had been able to say it. Then he added with a grin, "I just feel like I should tell ya that, I guess."

"Well," Rennie smiled, "I'm flattered. You really mean a lot to me too, Phantom."

They smiled for a good long second at one another. Both of them knew the words were true before they were ever spoken. Now that the words had been set free from their thoughts into the cool mountain air, it didn't feel like anything had to change. Like they would naturally seep into the fabric of the rest of their days together. So they got in the truck, coasted down the hill, and ended the day with burgers at Denny's.

CHAPTER

Unjustified

(n.) Text in columns where the individual lines do not all align.

"HI THERE, MR. PHANTOM. Hope you're having a good weekend. You're probably out today. I'll give you a try tomorrow."

I left the voicemail just as I often did. I knew he was like a kid on summer vacation. Only an empty stomach or nightfall would lure him back inside. I tried him a few more times after work and again on Sunday evenings, our unspoken weekly appointment, for two more weeks without an answer. So I started calling at odd times to try to catch him, midnight his time, 5:00 a.m., 3:00 p.m. No answer. Maybe he was on a long camping trip or went to visit a friend or something.

I didn't let my thoughts wander to worst-case scenarios, but that next week I kept Phantom's phone ringing every chance I got. While I sat at a stoplight, brushed my teeth, walked in to work, and washed the dishes, I tried him again and again. I pictured his cheap, landline phone ringing, ringing, ringing to no one in his apartment. The noise bouncing off the lime green walls, with its displays of meticulously crafted fishing flies, paintings accentuated with a touch of glitter glue, and photos of the inhabitant's latest trout—the habitat he had described to me during one of our first phone calls. I pictured his coffee table workbench buried under the ingredients of his latest project alongside a coffee can brimming with cigarette butts.

I wanted to catch the next flight west to check up on him, but imagining how the editor at my new job would react to an unplanned week off work was enough to talk me out of that idea. So I sat at my laptop and tried every online avenue I could think of to contact him. I typed "Sierra Phantom" into the search bar, then "J.P. Glover," and finally "John P. Glover."

Several photos of him popped up in one search with captions indicating they were taken by a guy named Travis Young. I searched again, now for that name, and found an email address. I sent him a message asking whether he was still in touch with the mountaineer captured in his photos.

I thought to call the local hospital to ask if he was on the patient list. "No one by the name Glover or Sierra Phantom," the woman answered.

I searched for his name over and over again, hunting for any blog posts or newspaper clippings about his whereabouts. I couldn't admit to myself that I was scanning the screen for an obituary or a police report. With each page of search results and each phone call, my mind and heart raced just as they did when I was rushing to gather information on breaking news. After more unfruitful attempts, I slammed my laptop shut in frustration and paced the living room. I wasn't a reporter trying to find a source. This wasn't about a writing assignment. It wasn't a missed deadline, an upset editor, a missed pay raise, or a trivial article that hung over my head. It was more than any of that. He was more than any of that.

Before I talked myself out of it, I gave it one last try. I sat back down at the kitchen table, opened my laptop, and typed in Phantom's address. He'd given it to me during our first phone call, so I could send him a few of my newspaper clips. The name and number for his apartment complex popped up. I dialed the number and held my breath. A woman named Elizabeth answered and said she was the apartment manager. "This was it," I thought. "She'll know."

I did my best to explain that I was a friend of the man who lived in Apartment 14 and that I hadn't been able to reach him for three weeks now. "Have you seen him?" I asked.

"No, I haven't seen him for a few weeks either." She sounded as though she didn't know much more than I did. "We've all been worried about him."

I didn't want to admit anything, so I kept the thought to myself: Sierra Phantom was the kind of guy who would pedal up to his favorite Sierra vista and quietly exit this life.

I finally found words that sounded more hopeful than I felt. "Can I give you my number, and when you hear from him, will you please give me a call?"

"Oh yes, sounds good. And please call me if you hear anything before me."

"OK, for sure. Thank you."

One week later, while I was at work, I noticed a missed call on my cell phone. It was from a 760 area code, same as Phantom's, and whoever it was had left a voicemail. I forced myself to wait until I got home from work to listen to it. I was nervous for the type of news that might be delivered in that twenty-second message. As soon as I pulled into my driveway, I hit "play." "Hello, Danielle. I understand you want to know what's going on with Sierra Phantom. Give me a call, and I'll give you the update."

I wondered if that was a friend or a nurse or a government worker. I didn't think she'd use his nickname if she was a woman calling in any official capacity. The voice sounded different, softer and friendlier, than the apartment manager's. I made my way inside the house and called her back.

"Hello, this is Rennie."

"Hi. This is Danielle. I just got your message."

"Oh, yes. Hi Danielle. Elizabeth at the apartments told me what you were working on. Phantom mentions you from time to time . . ."

"Mentions. Present tense," I thought. "That's promising."

"So let me tell you how he's doing. He's back in Bishop now at the care center recovering."

"Recovering? Recovering from what?"

"Oh, OK . . . well, Phantom came down with pneumonia. I think maybe because he kept going out, hiking, and fishing . . ." I noticed she called him Phantom, not Sierra Phantom or Mr. Glover. And she said it just as easily as if it were John. "He was in the hospital three days and kept getting worse until he went into a coma. I don't really know what triggered it. He was medivacked to Reno, and doctors are now saying he had septicemia, which is like a blood infection. A long time ago he had a third of his stomach removed, and I think that caused the infection . . ."

Her voice could only be described as kind. It was high-pitched, which almost made it sound upbeat, despite the somber message it was delivering. She spoke each word slowly and deliberately, with care.

"So is he OK now?" I began my usual circular pace around the house, from the living room to the dining room to the kitchen and back again.

"Well, let me backtrack a bit more."

"He was in a coma for a week in Reno. I guess they gave him a lot of antibiotics, and he came through it. Then he was on a ventilator for a week. Ed, his fishing buddy, and I heard the doctors were going to pull the plug and just let him go, so we got up there as quickly as we could. We rushed up to one of the doctors, and while we were still catching our breath, he asked whether anyone would care if they let him go. 'Yes,' we told him. Ed said that he'd become like the mascot of Bishop. And I told him, 'Ya know, Phantom is a real big fighter. If he had a chance to live, he would want to live.'"

I bit my bottom lip. I'd never been fully convinced that he was in his eighties. His voice, coarse and assured, let on that he had the energy of a person half that age. Right then, I realized I had always pictured him as that ageless man in his stories. The stories that had carried me so far from my kitchen table, to downtown Seattle, to the arctic plains of Alaska to the hiking trails of Rock Creek Canyon, and the quiet waters of the Owens River.

My pacing slowed as my eyes filled with tears.

She continued, "So, that changed the doctor's mind. But, you know, he's been doing a lot better this week. They were actually able to take him off the respirator Monday, and he can sit up now. They shaved his face, and he's pretty upset about that. Said, 'I've been growin' that for fourteen years.'" She laughed a sympathetic laugh and said, "Poor guy."

"So he can talk?"

"He's really hard to understand because they lost his dentures," she sighed. "I'm told when they flew him back into Bishop, he didn't have them in, so they must've lost them in Reno. I've been on the phone since Tuesday trying to find his teeth. Anyway, so they took him off antibiotics now and have him on a feeding tube. He seems stronger every day I visit him," she paused as if she were taking a moment to either smile or cry. "He's just not ready to go."

I thanked her for taking the time to call and fill me in, and just as I began to say goodbye, she asked, "Has he read what you've written?"

"No. I wasn't planning to share it with him until I was further along." "I think he'd like to read it," she nudged.

"Well, I can email you what I have. Can you get it to him?"

"Oh yes, of course. But I don't have email. I can give you my address." "That works."

I uncrumpled a grocery store receipt on our coffee table and jotted it down. I let her know I didn't want to bother her, but if she wouldn't mind keeping me updated on his progress, I'd appreciate it.

"Oh, you're no bother. I think it's great what you're doing. Phantom has done so much for this community; I think people need to know about it."

"Oh, yeah?" I knew about his guided tours and the community garden, but she made it sound like there might be more to it.

"You know, he's helped a lot of people in this town. He gives all his fish away, and he fixes up old reels and rods and gives them to the special needs adults at this group home in town. He makes sure everyone is taken care of with what little he has." She sounded like she was speaking through a smile, "I just think he's one in a million."

We finally said our goodbyes and agreed to talk again soon. And then I got to breaking Journalism Rule #4: don't show a source your work before it's published.

This is a rule of journalism ethics. If a source doesn't like how they or their company or their political party are portrayed in an article, they may coerce the journalist into changing it. Then the journalist has lost all objectivity.

I seemed to forget about this rule as I printed the unedited pages I'd written about Phantom's earliest years: his near escape from a pair of nuns, his success at the May Day swim meet, his precarious journey across Lake Washington in a leaky boat, his shoplifting stint, and the time he drank himself sick.

I used the last of my ink cartridge and slipped eighty-seven unstapled sheets of paper into a manila envelope. On top, I taped a photo of my husband, Aaron, and me in front of a waterfall in Thailand—I realized Phantom never knew what I looked like—and a Christmas card.

"Mr. Sierra Phantom, you've been in my thoughts and prayers. I hope you're feeling stronger every day. I look forward to the next time we can talk. I hope you can enjoy the holiday season, even though you're not able to fish. I'm sure you'll be out on the water soon . . ."

There, I broke Journalism Rule #5: be likable; don't like.

The best reporters are winsome, yet they are able to keep their opinions of people—as well as their politics, religion, and almost everything else—to themselves, for the most part. It makes sense. If a reporter becomes too close with the police chief or the school superintendent, then he or she will have a tough time covering all they do, both good and bad, in an honest light. For that matter, the same problem arises if a reporter obviously despises someone, say, the governor. Readers who love, hate, or are indifferent toward him all need to know they can trust the person who is delivering the information about him.

For the first time in a writing assignment, I happily jumped over this ethical barricade. I cared about Sierra Phantom. I was rooting for him. I had come to cherish not only his story but also who he was. I couldn't pinpoint exactly when it happened, but at some point in our talks, he must have moved from a source to something more. I've never sent a source a Christmas card.

CHAPTER

Advocacy Journalism

(n.) A type of journalism in which journalists openly take sides on an issue and express their opinions in reporting.

IT WAS ONE OF THOSE SIGHS that has little to do with breathing, pulling in needed oxygen and pushing out carbon dioxide. It was about releasing something more than air. It was exhaustion and sadness that Rennie exhaled when I called her two days later to check in and asked her, "How's he doing?"

"Oh, Danielle, he's not doing too well." She allowed herself a deep breath in and another sigh. "After we talked the other day, the doctors told me he has pneumonia and lung cancer. Yesterday they told me it was probably his last night, but he made it through the night, and he's still able to talk this morning."

I stopped my pacing and stayed quiet for a moment before asking, "How are you doing, Rennie?"

"Oh, I'm fine. Just tired. Ed and I tried to go to his apartment to get some of his stuff, but they taped it off. We could see inside that he'd left everything just as it was. It looked like he just stepped out to run a quick errand. Food was on the counter, a basket of laundry was on the floor, and a half-finished fly was in a vise on his coffee table. Did he tell you he made his own fishing flies?"

"Yes, he told me a lot about that."

"Good . . ." her voice trailed off a moment. "You know, I was thinking, if he does pass away, will you finish writing his story?"

I involuntarily winced as if I'd been kneed in the stomach. That was the first she'd put words to what we both feared, that Phantom might not make it. Instantly I wished she hadn't said it. I still pictured him as a sturdy outdoorsman already making plans for his next hike, just needed a couple weeks to down a few more cans of Ensure and heal up. For some reason my mind went to the Associated Press Stylebook, the Bible of grammar usage for news print. It insists publications write that a person died, not that he or she passed away or had left this life. What a callous rule. Whoever made such a heartless decision certainly didn't consult anyone who'd just lost a friend.

I stared blankly out the window until my eye caught a cardinal landing on our little dogwood tree; the friendly bird looked even more crimson in the forefront of the snow-covered backyard. I shook my head and quickly tried to refocus on what Rennie was really asking: Would I finish telling Phantom's story?

"Rennie . . ." I started.

"Yes, Danielle. Have you thought about that?"

"I'll finish it. Definitely," I made the promise to myself simultaneously. "I may need some help filling in a few of the holes, though. Maybe I can interview you and Ed and some of Phantom's other friends if you think they'd be up for that."

"I think everyone is so happy to know that Phantom's story, who he is and who he was, will be told, that we'll help you anyway we can."

"Great. Well, I'll save my questions for now," I said, suddenly realizing that I'd better ask Phantom what I could of my long list of unanswered questions. I didn't even know who taught him how to tie a fly or what he hauled around in his 60-pound backpack all those years. "Do you think Phantom would feel up to talking to me?"

"Oh, yes," her tone grew hopeful. "Maybe that's the nudge he needs to come out of this. Now, he doesn't have a phone, and the nurses around here aren't very helpful, but if you call the nurses station and ask very sweetly, they'll bring the phone to his bed."

"The nurses must be pretty awful," I thought. Rennie didn't seem like the type of person to say a harsh word about anyone who wasn't. "Well, I'll give it a shot," I said. She suggested I call in the evening when the nurses weren't as busy.

"So, he has pneumonia and lung cancer?" I asked in disbelief.

"Yes," she said softly. "I'm not too surprised about the lungs, I must say. Do you know he's smoked since he was a kid?"

"He told me he smoked but never said for how long."

"Well, last night he said, 'I think I'll stop smoking,'" she said it in a deep voice, an exaggerated impression of her friend. "I just laughed because he's always smoked these Paiute Smokes—he gets them from the reservation—and he'd say," she transitioned to his voice again, "'Don't you know they're good for you? They're all natural. They don't even need a filter.'"

I followed her lead and laughed with her. It sounded like she needed an excuse to smile.

"Whew, he's a funny guy. Oh, but we had a good night last night," she added.

"Really?" I had pictured her sitting at his deathbed amid grouchy nurses delivering ice chips for him and Jell-O for her.

"Oh, we did. Well, we just kept talking to one another, thinking it was our last night to hang out." She said this as though she were talking about a high school pal. "At first it was like we were kids whose parents were making one of us move. Ya know? I brought a bunch of photos of us and a few of his friends from fishing trips, and we talked about our favorite days together. He asked me what he's been missing out on lately, and I admitted to him that I saw the new Sherlock Holmes movie without him. I told him, 'I couldn't wait, and I needed something to cheer me up.' He joked, 'Well, ya owe me a night at the movies then.'"

She laughed. "It was just a sweet time to reflect."

"It seems like you two are great friends," I added softly.

"Oh yes. Ya know, we've never really talked much about our relationship. We never had to say we cared for one another. But last night, just sort of out of the blue, Phantom said, 'You know, Rennie, if I would've met you earlier, you would've been my mountain maiden.' It was so sweet." She let out another sigh, softer than the others. "I didn't want to scare him by crying, but I couldn't help it. Tears ran down my face, and I told him, 'You know I love you, Phantom.' And he said, 'Love you too, Rennie.' We've never spoken like that before. Last night,

I think we both just wanted to make sure the other person knew how much we cared."

There wasn't a thing I wanted to say to ruin the moment. I wrapped up our call by thanking her for sharing all of this, and I told her I'd give Phantom a call later that evening.

MY HANDS SHOOK as I dialed the number for Bishop Care Center. I was more nervous than the first time I had called Phantom more than two years earlier. My feet, in slippers, started their usual pace, shuffling along the hardwood floor from the living room to the kitchen and back again.

I was scared he would think I was going too far now, bugging him on his deathbed, just to hear a story. I wanted to tell him it was about much more than that now, and as the phone rang, I prayed I'd have the chance. "Hi, I am a friend of J.P. Glover, who I believe is in room 210." Rennie had given me his room number. "I know he doesn't have a phone in his room, and I know you all are extremely busy, but do you have a quick minute to bring him the phone? I won't keep him long." "OK, sure," the nurse said with ease.

I hadn't thought about what I would say if I got past the presumably ornery nurses who manned the phone. I flipped open my notebook and scribbled a few questions I needed to ask him if he sounded strong enough. I needed to know who had taught him to fish, and I wanted to hear more about the people in Bishop whom he'd helped over the years and what he wanted to do after—"H-h-hello"—my thoughts were interrupted by the word, delivered painfully in a voice I didn't recognize.

"Hi, Mr. Phantom. It's Danielle," I sped through my introduction. "I don't want to bug you, but I just want to say 'hi' and let you know I'm praying for a quick recovery."

"Danielle. . .Hi," He just barely articulated the words through the receiver. They sounded more like a painful exhale than a greeting. I would've never guessed that he was the one speaking unless he'd said my name. Rennie warned me he would be difficult to understand without his teeth, but she didn't say he was so weak.

Over our years of talks, I was always the one who brought our conversations to an end and asked that we pick them up the following Sunday. He could have talked all week if I had the time to listen. With the time difference, it was usually well past my bedtime when he'd wrap up his stories. But this time, he was the one who was tired. It was the first time since I'd known him that he didn't launch into some grand tale. I immediately felt awful for taking some of the last of his energy. But he was the one who apologized.

"I'm . . . so sorry," he released each word slowly.

"Sorry?" I said softly. "You don't need to be sorry about anything."

"I'll work hard . . . to get better," he took a raspy breath and carried on, "so we can finish."

"Phantom, don't worry about that. Your friend, Rennie, got in touch with me, and she's going to connect me with Ed and your other friends. They've said they'll help me pick up where we left off," involuntary tears filled my eyes. "We've got it covered. Just rest."

"OK," he whispered. He said something else, but I couldn't understand him, and I wasn't going to make him repeat it. I attempted to sign off as upbeat as he always did, but this time I spoke his farewell phrase. "Have a swinging safari, Mr. Phantom. Talk to you soon."

He died ten hours later. Rennie's number flashed on my cell phone the following day. I feared the news on the other line, so I stood up and walked out of my cubicle to the parking lot. "Hi, Rennie."

"He's gone," she said bravely, as if she was all out of tears. "He fell asleep this morning. Were you able to talk to him?"

"Yes," I said through quiet tears. "Last night."

"Oh I'm so thankful, Danielle." She took a deep breath and continued, "Ed and I were talking. We want to put an obituary in the newspaper, but neither of us write very well. So, we thought of you. Would you be willing to write it?"

"Wait, what? Really?" I was taken off guard that they would trust me with this. They had never even met me, and I never technically met Sierra Phantom.

"Yes, would you?" she added.

"Rennie, I'd be honored. I'll write it as soon as I'm off work. I'll get it to you first thing tomorrow morning. Can I get your email address? Let me grab a pen . . . "

"I don't have email. I don't even have a computer. I'm a bit behind the times," she laughed subtly.

"Oh yeah." I'd forgotten.

"But the manager of my trailer park does. You can send it to her, and I'll just have her print it off and run it down to The Register."

"No worries. That should work just fine." She gave me the address. "Great. Thanks, Rennie." I let an uncomfortable silence settle over the line as I thought about what I could do to offer my condolences. I wanted to tell her how sorry I was that she'd lost her best friend. But she didn't seem in the mood to dwell on it, as though she had too much on her to-do list to make time to grieve. So I didn't say anything about it; instead, I just asked, "Can I call you sometime soon so you can help me fill in some gaps about Phantom?"

"Oh, yes. Give me a few weeks to get everything settled around here. I'll tell you about the first time I met Phantom," she sounded like she was smiling now. "For now, let's just say it starts with us on a road trip to LA and him telling me story and after story—he was like my own personal book on tape."

I laughed with her, "I believe that. Can't wait."

But as soon as I had the obituary written that night, I stopped any writing about Phantom. It was as if I mentally, or maybe emotionally, couldn't. I tried to one morning before work, but I felt stuck. As if

I were attempting to navigate a wilderness without my guide, my knowledgeable, quirky guide.

I tried to put any writing, and put him, out of my thoughts as best I could. Over the previous year, I had only mentioned to a few close friends that I was interviewing an old man on the other end of the continent, so I told myself it'd be easy to replace our Sunday evening talks with some other routine and to crowd out dreams of high-altitude adventure with humdrum distractions of my suburban life. And it was, for a while.

One of my friends who knew I had been talking regularly with a man who'd lived much of his life in the wild called one day just to chat, and she asked me how our talks were going. I told her what had happened and about my last conversation with Phantom. Saying aloud that I had promised him I'd somehow find and tell the rest of his story was an unwelcome reminder.

"I don't know quite how I'll do that," I sighed into the phone and then slightly changed the subject. "It was hard to hear him that day. He sounded like a completely different person. Usually, he was so full of excitement and energy, like a kid at Disneyland," I took another deep breath and concluded all I had to say with, "Ugh, it just sucks."

"Yeah, it does," Zoe offered. "Sorry, Danielle." We both stayed quiet for a second; then she added, "You know, their stories are especially important to them."

"Who's that?"

I had told her a while ago about Phantom's childhood. I thought she'd be interested to hear it because at the time she was working as a social work intern, supporting homeless kids and orphans who'd been shuffled throughout the state by way of California's foster care system.

"Foster children," she continued. "They are known for their storytelling. Because they're moved from family to family and house to house, there's no one who holds all of who they are, from beginning to end." She paused, giving me space to respond, but I didn't take it. "A life story is a person's mark on the world."

"Yeah, I see what you mean," I added softly.

"You carry part of Sierra Phantom's narrative, Danielle, maybe more of it than anyone else."

As her words settled, I felt even more inadequate. All I had done was write down what he had been willing to share with me. I was ashamed to think I'd never even shaken the man's hand. I furrowed my eyebrows and said, "I don't know about any of that, Zoe."

"Well, OK but—"

"The people he did life with carry his story," I continued. "Like his friend, Rennie; the guys he fished with; his neighbors; his favorite servers at Denny's; even the people who looked at him sideways when they saw his long beard and cowboy hat covered in fishing lures," I rattled all this off more to myself than Zoe. Then, I suddenly paused.

"What are you thinking?" she broke the silence. "I've got to get to Bishop."

J.P. 'Sierra Phantom' Glover
1926-2012

John P. Glover died Monday, Jan. 30, 2012, at the Bishop Care Center. He was 85.

Those who knew Glover did not call him by his birth name – most never knew it. He was known as the Sierra Phantom, a nickname earned after living 50 years in the wilderness of the Sierra Nevada Mountains.

Glover was born in Orange, Calif., on July 20, 1926, to Eric and Heidi Glover, who both died when he was a toddler. He endured an unstable childhood, moving between orphanages and foster homes every few years throughout California and Washington. At 16 years old, he lied about his age to join the U.S. Navy with an itch to discover the world. He served as a World War II sharpshooter in Alaska for four years. By the age of 21, the anguish of his childhood and the war drove Glover to choose a life as a lone mountaineer. He set up inconspicuous camps throughout the High Sierra and lived apart from civilization, only visiting small mountain towns every few months to replenish his supplies.

In his early 70s, Glover moved into an apartment in Bishop, where he quickly became a local legend. He was often spotted sitting outside Erik Schat's Bakkerÿ and Raymond's Deli, tying his self-invented glitter flies for fishing.

Glover also served as a mountain and fishing guide, a job he saw as an opportunity to pass along all he had learned in the wilderness to the generations that followed.

Glover will be remembered for his tales of survival in the wild, his ability to make fast friends with anyone willing to lean in and hear those tales, and the philosophy which he lived by – you're never lonely when you're surrounded by nature.

A memorial service is being planned by friends for a later date.

CHAPTER

Kicker

(n.) The closing paragraph of a story which often contains a call to action.

I KNEW THE WORDS were true as soon as I spoke them, but I couldn't help but count the cost. I went back and forth about whether to really go, to spend four hundred bucks on a flight, to convince my editor to give me a week off work, and to stay with people I'd never met to complete a project for which I still felt unequipped. It would mean I was all in. For weeks, the decision sat as the backdrop to all of my other thoughts. Some moments I swore I had more to lose if I stubbornly kept up this unpaid quest to understand a man who felt more like an illusion.

As I sat on the edge of sleep one night, subconsciously mulling it over again, the advice of my first editor came to me: the best stories are found outside of the newsroom. "Well, there's my answer," I thought as I surrendered to sleep. It was decided.

One month later, I sat in a cramped coach seat, steadying a plastic cup of cranberry juice. As I watched the mini red waves of juice created by the sporadic rhythm of turbulence that comes with flying thirty-five thousand feet above civilization, I thought about what might await me at the other end of the flight.

The months following Phantom's death had been a whirlwind of online research and phone calls as I worked to piece together what more I could about him from a distance. I contacted every person I could find who had any connection to him, and some of those contacts led me to others whose paths had somehow crossed with his. I started each conversation the same, by introducing myself and asking, "Would you be willing to share your version of Sierra Phantom?"

At the start of almost every interview, those who knew him best humbly stated they had nothing to offer to his tale. That so-and-so "would really have more to say" because he or she had known him longer, talked to him more, lived closer, or had more in common with him. They always said they'd be happy to give me so-and-so's phone number, and it went on from there.

But I knew that each of them had something important to offer. It was as if, just as everyone has his or her own interests and personality, each of Phantom's friends and admirers was drawn to a different part of him. Vets heard of his experiences in the war, those he was willing to share; fishermen quizzed him on all he knew about snagging wild trout; pure outdoorsmen learned of his years navigating the High Sierra; others were drawn to his generous heart. Even those who had only passed him on Main Street on their way to somewhere more important carried a piece of him. "I always thought he was just a bullshitter, ya know with all his stories," one honest high school kid told me. "But he was always really nice to everyone."

The most exciting find was Lauren. I don't know how she found her, but Rennie called me one day to pass along the phone number of a woman who'd known him in the early '60s, when he was about my age and living the kind of life that branded him as Sierra Phantom. Much of the verifying I felt obligated to do about this story, she satisfied in our first phone call.

"I met him when I was about ten years old. He was friends with my grandmother, and I got to know him because I lived with her in the summers." She announced all of this matter-of-factly, as if she was well aware she was a rare living witness to the young mountaineer some locals now doubted. "One of his camps was set up a couple of miles from Grandma Louise's cabin, so they'd run into one another and got to be close…"

She talked loud and fast as though she was in the middle of something and couldn't spare much time to chat. But after an hour on the phone with her, I realized she was talking quickly because she had so much to share about the legend of a man who was such an important part of her childhood. "He was a really nice looking young man. He was very warm and kind—a gentle man. You always felt safe and secure around him."

She said that they went forty years without seeing one another. She thought maybe he'd disappeared into the mysterious crannies of the Sierra

Nevada range and would never be seen again. But breakfast at Denny's changed that.

"… It was quite the reunion. Now whenever we're in Bishop, we spend every moment with him. Well, we did," she paused a second. "Our trips revolved around him. Who could ever get enough of that greatness of presence? … This next trip is going to be very different. It'll be tough."

She asked if I had found people in Bishop to be helpful.

"Oh, yes," I told her, mentioning that people wanted to honor Phantom but a lot hesitated to offer their take on him, simply because they didn't want to stand in a spotlight meant for their friend. "One of his good friends is letting me stay at her place and has offered to show me around."

"He was so dearly loved," she sighed. "That's why the town has opened the locked gate to you. That's not the new Bishop." I didn't know what she meant by that. "The new Bishop is all about attracting tourists and the money they bring. But the old Bishop is what you're getting, welcoming, loving. Like Phantom."

Travis, the photographer student I'd emailed when Phantom was missing, got back to me a couple of weeks before my flight. "Ah man, I'll just miss you," he said when I told him the dates I'd be in town. "I'll be in Utah. But listen, while you're there, you've got to get some hiking in. Do you have a hike picked out?"

"No," I said honestly. "I hadn't really thought about that."

"Well, there's one along the first alpine shelf out of the valley . . ." I jotted down his directions for a route that circled a series of lakes and offered views of the expansive valley I'd heard so much about. "That's a classic Sierra Phantom hike."

Rennie got me in touch with Ed, and I called him asking pages of questions about Phantom's fishing techniques, how he came up with his glitter flies, whether he sold many of them, and if they really worked. Ed answered what questions he could, but he said a lot of what he now knew about his friend he'd heard in the few weeks after his death from people who knew him only briefly.

"People are comin' outta the woodwork," he said the first time I called him. Through emails, phone calls, and blog posts, he'd heard and read story after story of fishermen, from beginners to pros, who had bumped into this aging fishing expert along the water who offered advice that sent them away with more fish than they could haul home. "This is the guy I've been fishing with for all this time, and I didn't even know who he really was. He's caught thousands of people's interest."

As if overwhelmed by the outpouring of love and respect for his friend, Ed told me he didn't feel he could accurately portray Phantom. "I don't know," he said when I started down my list of questions. "There are so many others who've known him longer than I have."

Even Rennie encouraged me to focus my interviews on others; those longtime Bishop folks would have a lot to say about him. "I don't know how much I can really offer," she said gently. But she was more than willing to help me get out to Bishop where I could find others to complete the story.

A week before my flight, I got a card in the mail from her. It had a beautiful watercolor painting of a High Sierra lake on the cover and held a folded sheet of paper ripped from a notebook with a message that assured me she was eager to offer her help. It read in her cursive: "Inyo County Idiot's Guide to High-Class Camping," and it was followed by a list of must-bring items, including shorts, T-shirts, sweats, jeans, and a cool-weather jacket. "Temperatures can range from thirty-five to one hundred degrees up here, but don't worry, it's a DRY heat," she assured me with a penned smiley face. "Just bring these things and a smile, and we'll have lots of fun!" I could hear her soft, cheery voice through the fluid loops and curves of the black ink. "I'm so excited to meet you and show you around."

We called one another almost every night in those final days before my trip, excitedly finalizing details, like what lakes I should visit, where we would eat, and wherever and whoever else she felt I should see to glean everything I needed to know about Sierra Phantom and the place he came to call home. "Oh, we'll have such a good time. I wish Phantom were around to join us," she said one night, and then she quickly moved on to the next sentence, not allowing herself to dwell on his absence. "Can I ask you something?"

"For sure," I said.

"Well, you know so much about me; tell me more about you. How old are you?"

"I'm thirty, but people say I look twenty, which I hate," I said, laughing a little.

"Are you married?"

"Yes, his name is Aaron. We've been married five years now."

"So, what's Aaron think of all this, you coming out here by yourself to hang out with a bunch of goofy Bishop people?"

"You know, actually, he seems fine with it. My mom is the one who's worried. But I told her, 'Rennie's great, I'll be fine.'"

She laughed, "I have to tell you, my son, Mark, is the one who is worried on this end. He said, 'I don't know about letting a stranger come spend a week here. You've never met this woman.'"

"Hah, really?" I laughed with her.

"I told him, 'I promise you, she's sweet.'"

"So I guess everyone is worried about this except us, huh?"

"Sounds like it," she said and let out a final sigh that was half giggle. "Oh, we'll have so much fun. Just tell your mom and Aaron that you're in good hands. We'll take good care of you."

Now in flight toward California, I smiled as I thought back on our last conversation. I dug out the now wrinkled "Idiot's Guide" from my backpack and set it on the tray table as a bit of comfort, or maybe proof, that she and the others I'd gotten to know by phone were waiting for me at the other end of the flight. In the months between Phantom's death and my trip to Bishop, it was those distant voices, three time zones and fifteen states away, that had become my partners in this project. A project they cared as deeply about as I did.

Already, I felt I had gotten to know the reluctantly retired mountaineer better through conversations with his friends, others who he'd lured in. I discovered that it wasn't his flashy, or arguably gaudy, appearance, or even his wildest stories, that drew the best of his friends. It was all the parts of him that were unexaggerated. It was his heart that brought me to this point. I wasn't on a typical West Coast vacation. I had set out to get to know a man by the words he'd left behind. I was on that adventure he'd promised to deliver years earlier.

I laid my head back on the faux leather plane seat and let my eyes, still heavy from the 5:00 a.m. wake-up call, drift out the window. I mindlessly watched the beige plains sweep beneath us until I let my eyes fall shut.

"Can I take that?" a stewardess interrupted. She displayed a plastic smile as she started toward my empty cup.

"Yes, thank you."

She chucked it in a white garbage bag. "And that?" she asked gesturing toward the "Idiot's Guide."

"Oh, no. No, I need this."

"Any trash?" she continued down the row.

I laid my head back in its place to see jagged, snow-capped peaks now filling the tiny window. "Now, these look like the High Sierra," I thought, wondering how far we might be from Bishop. Snow hung on to each elevated crest but seemed to have surrendered to July heat in the dips of the landscape.

It looked like the surface of the moon. Pure from any human influence, as if streetlights, Kmarts, coffee shops, and even people were in another existence. But I caught myself studying every visible nook among the grand peaks, looking for a dot of a man, a mountaineer, scaling the sharp terrain just for fun.

CHAPTER

Dateline

(n.) A city or geographic name of a story's origin.

IT WAS THE FAMILIAR SCOTTISH ACCENT of my college friend that greeted me when I stepped out of the terminal of Meadows Field Airport. Craig, who had first convinced me to write about the "wild man" he'd met while hiking three years earlier, offered to drive me from Bakersfield to Bishop.

"MacMurchy!" I heard my maiden name shouted from the airport pickup line. I looked down the queue of idling cars to spot a tall blond waving from the driver's seat of a Toyota truck. He hurried out, gave me a hug, tossed my bag in the truck bed and climbed back into the cab before two security officers blowing referee whistles and telling people to, "keep moving," could bark in our direction.

"Thanks for the ride," I said as I buckled my seatbelt and settled in for the four-hour drive.

"Are you kidding? I got you into this whole thing in the first place," he laughed.

"This is true," I added dryly, and we got to catching up about where life had taken each of us since the college days of late-night cram sessions, ultimate Frisbee Fridays and tailgate parties.

AFTER HOURS OF VOID, the lush green of a golf course was blinding. The Bishop Golf Club on the far south side of town was the sudden indication that travelers had reached their sought-after oasis.

"Hey there, Rennie. We just pulled into town," I pronounced in my cell phone with nervous excitement. She reciprocated the greeting with her own blend of eager nerves. "I just realized, I was so excited to get here I never got your address."

I dug for a pen and a crinkled receipt from my purse and gave her the, "OK, ready."

"So you're on Main Street?"

"Yeah, looks like we're passing a BBQ Bills on the left . . ." I motioned to Craig to turn down the country music he had insisted serve as the soundtrack for our road trip.

"Take the first left after Schat's Bakkerÿ. You'll see it pretty soon here. And you're there."

I laughed and returned the receipt and pen to my purse. "Well, that's easy. See ya in a minute."

At that, I spotted the bakery. I had pictured a quaint shop with a mom-and-pop feel, but it was a two-story brick building the size of a Walgreens. It had the look of something you'd see in the little towns of Germany, with blue clay roof shingles and a stained glass window near the entrance depicting a cartoon version of Erick Schat himself holding a tray of goodies. The patio squeezed in a dozen tables and a couple of kids' twenty-five-cent rides, all of it occupied. Huge signs beckoned the few who did not already know a stop was practically involuntary: "World Famous Original Sheepherder Bread ~ Established 1903."

It was all enough to upstage the narrow entrance to the J Diamond Mobile Home Ranch, a freshly paved single-lane road nearly hidden behind the six-foot fence that defined the bakery's property.

"I think that's it," I directed Craig a half-second too late. "Whoopsie," he said as he jerked the truck into the next parking lot and whipped us around with speed.

He reined in the truck to a coast as we entered the mobile home park. Then, he jolted us to a dead stop and shut off the "Folsom Prison Blues" to let us take in the scene. A little boy surfed the narrow road on a skateboard. Hovering three inches above the pavement, he passed four, nine, then twenty something homes before he U-turned to make the fleeting ride again. Without realizing it, our eyes went down the line of homes at his same pace. Some of the homes had wheels, ready to relocate at any moment, and others sat in a semi-permanent state confined within a chain link fence.

We spotted a woman at the end of the line of homes with a big grin. She gave a small wave with her left hand and held a cane to the pavement with her right. I had forgotten that in one of our first conversations she had told me she had hip replacement surgery and her spine was missing cartilage, which kept her in pain a lot of the time. "Oh, it's old age. What can ya do?" she said, without a hint of complaining.

"There's Rennie," I pointed. The truck didn't move.

"I don't know about this," Craig said, looking up and down the row of trailer homes again.

I verbally nudged him to take his foot off the brake and go. "I'll be fine."

"Where are you sleeping?" He reluctantly returned the truck to a crawl toward Rennie. She stood at the end of a stretch of stark white trailers in front of a friendly, pale pink version, the only one with a mini garden just off the road. Tomatoes crawled up a chain link fence and left just enough soil for a half dozen California poppies.

"Well, I think in a tent or something," I said, trying to see how a tent might fit next to the trailer, occupying all but a few inches of its lot. "It'll be fine—hi, Rennie!" I waved my hand out Craig's window. He brought us to a stop and unlocked the doors to free me from the passenger seat.

Rennie took each step in a decisive manner, as if she saved her steps only for life's best stuff. My legs were stiff from the long drive, so we both hobbled to reach one another.

"It's so good to see you," she said, the words muffled through our hug. "You, too, Rennie."

"I feel like we're just picking up where we left off, like old friends," she smiled. She leaned back half a step to look me over as if to compare the real me to the one she'd pictured.

Despite the cane, she looked years younger than seventy-five. I would've guessed she was closer to sixty. I don't know if it was her energetic eyes, her brown hair (which she later revealed came compliments of a box of L'Oréal dye) or her buoyant spirit.

I introduced Rennie to Craig and told her he was eager to get back on the road. He wanted to stop by South Lake and get back to Bakersfield that night.

"You sure you don't want to stay for dinner?" she asked.

"Thank you, but I have to get back at a decent time to feed the chickens and sheep," Craig said.

"He's an Ag teacher," I explained.

"That's sweet of you to make this drive just to turn around again," she said. "Let me at least send you home with a snack. I baked cookies last night."

"Well, I won't turn that down," Craig said.

"Then I'll show you where you're staying, Danielle." She gestured to the opposite end of the park before she made her way up her porch steps and disappeared into the trailer.

As Craig lifted my heavy duffle bag to my shoulder, he whispered, "MacMurchy, if even for a second you don't feel safe or welcome or anything, call me. I'll come back to get you right away, all right?"

"I'll be fine," I half laughed. Rennie returned with a plastic baggie plump with chocolate chip cookies.

"Ooh, thank you," Craig said with big eyes. "You sure you can't stay a bit?" she tried again.

"I'm looking forward to getting another glimpse of South Lake," Craig said, his eyebrows raised at the thought of the lake. "That's where I met Sierra Phantom."

"Oh, you met Phantom?" Rennie smiled up at him.

"Yes, a buddy and I actually got to eat dinner with him. We listened to his stories for hours."

"That sounds about right," Rennie laughed.

"He left us just stunned. Really an incredible guy."

"Yes, he was," she smiled. "All right, well, have a swinging safari."

Craig grabbed my shoulder and yanked me toward him for the kind of hug you'd give a kid brother. "It was good to catch up with my old friend, anyway. See ya in a week," he said as he got back into the truck.

"OK, thanks for the ride. Dinner is on me before I fly home, OK?" "See ya, MacMurchy . . ." the Celtic garble faded as the truck pulled out of the park and onto Main Street.

"What a sweet guy," Rennie said with a sigh of satisfaction. "Now, let's get you settled in."

She nodded her head toward the opposite end of the park and began to gingerly walk in that direction. She led me past a long row of shoddy tin mailboxes, each displaying sticker numbers to indicate which home the mail inside belonged to, then slowly over a bridge that stretched across a small stream. She seemed to be leading me out of the neighborhood until she lifted her cane to point to a grassy area hidden behind the park's office. "Back there," she said and continued on. We came around the corner to see a camping tent large enough to sleep twenty of a person's closest friends. It rivaled the size of some of the trailer homes.

My chin dropped. "Oh my goodness, Rennie. It's huge."

"Mark helped me set it up," she said with a smile as she took a seat at the picnic table next to the tent. She gestured for me to go in without her. I unzipped the door, ready to plop my bag inside and begin discovering Bishop, but I paused when I saw what Rennie had made of the temporary dwelling.

"On the right of the door there, you should see a light switch," she directed from the picnic table.

"A light switch?" I tried to clarify. Sure enough, I flipped a switch, which was wired to a dome light in the center of the ceiling. I suddenly felt the need to leave my shoes at the entrance as the detail of the three-room tent came into view. One room, the living room, had a blow-up couch covered in a blanket and a throw pillow.

The room on the opposite end was made up like a bedroom with an overstuffed queen air mattress for a bed, fresh towels, and a miniature bottle of lotion on the pillow. A cooler next to the bed doubled as a nightstand, holding a Coleman lamp and a battery-operated clock. The third room was like a temporary office with a card table, flanked by two chairs; it all sat neatly on throw rugs. "I wanted to make sure you had your own space to work," Rennie later said. The table held another Coleman lamp and a gift basket of sorts brimming with enough supplies to camp in style for a month: cereal, cookies, bananas, plasticware, a coffee mug, wet wipes, Kleenex, a mirror, miniature shampoos, conditioners, soaps, and a map of Bishop.

"There's water and milk over ice in the ice chest," Rennie hollered from the picnic table.

I stepped out of the tent with no shoes and no words. I had met this woman ten minutes earlier, and she had prepared a mansion for me. I noticed the stream we'd passed created a three-foot waterfall just a few yards from my tent, and tall trees offered a rare shade over my temporary home. Even the cool grass on my bare feet offered its own kind of gracious greeting.

"I really feel bad that we don't have space for you in the trailer," Rennie started. She must've taken my silence as a bad thing. "I just hope this will do—"

"Rennie," I stopped her. "I have never felt so welcome."

CHAPTER

Shoe-leather Reporting

*(v.) An on-the-ground approach to journalism,
where reporters leave the safety and comfort of their
desks in search of the full story.*

BY SIX THE NEXT MORNING, I was in my makeshift office Rennie had set up, tapping out notes from the previous day on my laptop. The miniature waterfall that had helped me fall asleep the night before had awakened me early with the rude reminder that the nearest bathroom was a block away. This had me up in time to be one of the first in town to greet the California sunshine.

Rennie had told me the previous night that I was within walking distance of every one of Phantom's favorite Bishop hangouts. She reminded me that she was not a morning person, so I was welcome to set out on my own without her. Before I headed out for the day, I threw on a gray, casual skirt and a striped navy blue blouse that was one of my work staples. I peered into the hand mirror Rennie had included in my gift basket to put on just enough makeup to mask any sign I was temporarily living in a tent. I packed every pocket in my camera bag with everything I needed to chronicle who Sierra Phantom was and the town that seemed to bring him to life: a notebook, business cards, sunscreen, pens, cell phone, and of course a camera.

As I walked from my tent toward Main Street, the feeling I was about three hours short on sleep set in. "A coffee is a must," I thought as I guided my feet out of the trailer park and along the sidewalk toward Schat's.

It wasn't even 8:00 a.m., and already the place crawled with vacationers. I waited my turn before pushing through the heavy, wooden front doors to find I was crowded on all sides by German knickknacks and sweet treats. I meandered my way through their delicious maze and made it out relatively unscathed, with an apple fritter and a tall black coffee. I took a seat at the table on the front patio that Rennie had described as "his spot" and watched tourists push their way in and out of the bakery. I don't know how Phantom managed to get much done on his flies sitting here all day, with a steady stream of patrons and his need to personally greet each of them. People must've been his priority.

As soon as I devoured my fritter, I continued my walk down Main. "Bishop really is just as Phantom described it," I thought. A place trying to hold on to its past while giving in to just enough of the new to keep tourists coming. The Holiday Inns, Marriotts, and Ramada Inns took their turns between the Thunderbird Motel, Village Motel, and the Trees Motel, each of which had stood its ground for the better part of fifty years. Among the inns were well-used gas stations, a slew of sporting goods stores, a shiny new McDonalds, and a trendy coffee shop. Then, mom-and-pop shops appeared as a reminder of the small pioneer town Phantom first got to know.

I passed all this as I made my way to Mac's Sporting Goods. Rennie suggested I make it my first stop. "That's where Phantom got most of his supplies," she told me.

Mac's wasn't the kind of place that would catch most people's eye. The small building crouched in the shadow of the hefty Jack's Restaurant next door. It was simple and unassuming. Unlike the slew of other nearby sporting goods stores that boasted professional-looking displays in the window—in one, mannequins dressed in trendy Patagonia gear gathered around a Coleman tent, and another displayed a mock fishing scene depicting a man with a prize trout on the line—Mac's had no gimmicks to get customers in the door. It was the kind of place that drew only the most serious of fishermen.

Inside, the older man behind the counter chatted about the day's expected heat with a couple of men dressed for a day on the water, so I walked around the shop, surveying each of its aisles as if I were supplying my own fishing excursion. Whoever stocked this place was the kind of guy you would want to pack your vehicle before a move. Every inch of the narrow shop was put to good use. A rainbow of rubber worms that could easily be mistaken for candy hung perfectly aligned on half of the shop's walls. A line of fishing rods standing in patterned formation down the middle of the store divided the larger gear from the endless supply of lures. Shelves in the back of the store gave tourists a selection of souvenirs to remember their Sierra visit.

I held a T-shirt that read "BISHOP, Gateway To The High Sierra" up to my chest and turned toward a mirror squeezed between fishing nets. I carefully put it back in its place when I noticed the eyes of a dozen animals mounted on the wall; deer, antelope, and trout eyes followed me with each step as if they were decoys for a security system.

"Can I help you find something?" the man asked, now the only other person in the shop.

"Oh, hi," I said, startled. "Yes, well . . ." I started and stopped.

IF THERE'S ONE THING I have a talent for, it's easing people into sharing their story with me. On my best days, I can convince a politician to stray from his talking points about job creation to reveal what he really cares about, who he really is, and what's prompted him to want to make decisions on behalf of thousands, or even millions, of his neighbors. Journalists learn very quickly that a combination of winsome and cunning produces the most fruitful interviews. That sounds manipulative. And yes, sometimes it is. I have a deadline and an expectation I'm working toward. But I can honestly say that most often I want to know, not just need to know, the who, what, when, where, and how of people's stories. And I don't think it's by chance that it's the genuine conversations that open the gate for the best stories.

But this felt different than any on-the-clock meeting. Phantom's story was in my hands, and it wasn't just a day's paper that would lose out if I failed. I had never so desperately needed a string of interviews to go without a hitch as I did now.

"Hi there," I attempted to sound comfortable. "My name is Danielle, and I'm working on a book about Sierra Phantom. I'm told he stopped in here a lot." I handed the man, who looked in his late sixties, a business card that advertised my day job as a reporter.

He must've spotted the address on the card for my current job at a newspaper in Virginia because his face turned from a smile at the mention of one of his best customers to a skeptical grimace.

"East-Coaster, huh?" he asked, his grimace becoming an all-out sneer as he looked my outfit up and down. "Why are you coming clear up here to write a book about Sierra Phantom?"

Damn it. I lost him already, I thought.

I was often mistaken for a college kid, so I thought he'd take me more seriously with my business card in hand. I should've known better in Bishop. I should've just said what I honestly felt. I wanted him to know how much I care about Phantom. How I'd spent the months since his death tracking down any detail of his life that I could. How I'd drained a savings account to buy a flight. How I was taking the week unpaid to be in Bishop. How I slept in a tent the night before.

My shoulders tightened as I searched for the right words, or any words at this point. "I got to know Phantom through a friend who lives in Bakersfield—I'm not really an author; I'm a newspaper reporter—but when I heard all he'd done, I felt like someone should write a book about him." I paused. His sneer held, so I kept on, "I interviewed him over the phone almost every week. We really got close . . ."

No change, his eyes looked through me as if he were noting the need to stock more wiggly worms on the wall behind me. He leaned on the glass counter with both arms outstretched as though it were up to the counter to hold him upright after an exhausting day.

I started up again, softer and more slowly. "I want you to know, I didn't drop into Bishop to make money off Phantom. I'm here on my own dime, and I just wanted to get to know him more from the perspective of the people up here." I paused, and after seeing I had made little progress, I looked down at my feet in nervous frustration as if I were literally sinking. When I looked up, without a smile this time, I spoke the truest words I had yet, admitting my burden, "I promised him I would write his story."

"Hmm . . ." I couldn't tell if that was a good or bad hmm. He moved his weight from the counter to stand straight in his sturdy Red Wing boots.

"OK," he said; his eyes and his tone had softened. "What'd you say your name was?"

"Danielle."

He extended his hand to shake mine. "My name is Ron." His slight smile caused me to release a deep sigh. "I'm not the owner of Mac's, but I help manage it. I don't really think I have much I can offer you, but I'll see what I can do."

"Well, just in case, I'll ask you a couple questions." My lungs were still playing catch-up while my mind searched for how to begin. I pulled my notebook from my camera bag and plopped the rest of my gear at my feet.

I asked the surface questions first, like how often did Phantom stop in, what did he buy, and, really, how good of a fishermen was he.

"He caught fish; that's for sure. He knew all these lakes like the back of his hand. He knew every little inlet that some people who've fished here most their lives don't know. He knew where the fish were going to be and when," Ron nodded and smiled as if Phantom still impressed him to this day. "He'd stop in a few times a week, park his bike out front, and tell me where the fish were biting and how his Glitter Fly sales were going that week. I think he considered us sort of business partners because he'd buy supplies at our place, create his own flies, and sell them all along Main Street. And he was quick to send customers looking for more fishing supplies our way."

He said Phantom had been stopping in the store for more than ten years. Ron let him run a tab that he'd pay off at the end of each month.

"And according to him, he holds the world record for the largest brown trout ever caught. Says he caught it up at Long Lake forty years ago. That might be a stretch," he smiled and looked out the front window in a moment of thought. Then, he quickly looked back at me and added, "But who knows. We weren't there to disprove it."

The bell above the front door chimed, welcoming a trio of teenage boys. "I'll hang around a few more minutes," I told Ron. I scooped my camera bag off the floor and did another spin around the place. "How you boys doing?" Ron asked them in his big voice.

As soon as they left, I returned to my spot at the end of the counter display and picked up where we left off. "So, you think it was all true?" The words came out more abruptly than I'd meant them.

"Oh yeah," Ron said in a serious tone. "I know people who've known him for years and years, and knew him in his younger days when he was living in caves and tents and igloos. It's true. I don't know if all his little stories like the fishing records are for real, but he was a mountaineer in the truest sense of the word. He survived by himself up there winter, spring, summer, fall. That's the way he lived his life."

We both stood quietly for a moment, digesting the reality that we knew a man who was like no one else. Hearing Phantom tell his stories with such detail made them feel real, as though he really had climbed that mountain or escaped that avalanche or rescued those people from that blizzard. But they were so incredible, I often thought they couldn't be true.

"He was just a really neat guy," Ron nudged the moment along. "He really became like an icon in this town."

With that, I put my notebook back in my bag, thanked him, and told him to call me if he thought of anything else people should know about Sierra Phantom. Walking out, I sighed in relief and whispered, "Thank you, Lord."

My shoulders relaxed as I breathed in the dry mountain air from Main Street. I took my time walking along the sidewalk, and I pictured Sierra Phantom coasting along beside me on his squeaky Huffy, stopping in and looking for deals at the thrift stores, the diners, and the little shops.

Before I searched out my next interview, I made a quick pit stop. "What was I thinking?" I sighed to myself as I climbed back into the tent. I shoved my skirt and blouse to the bottom of my duffle bag and pulled out a pair of cut off shorts and a flannel shirt. I couldn't decide whether I was changing to feel closer to Phantom or to fit in better in Bishop. Probably both.

"BISHOP HAS A FEW DECENT SPOTS to eat," Rennie said as we caught up on her front porch after my first day of interviews.

For American fare at a good price, there was Jack's Restaurant and Jeff's Country Kitchen. Bar B-Q Bill's was the place for beef brisket and cornbread. Whiskey Creek was where the wealthier tourists went for steak and salmon. There was a hole-in-the-wall Mexican restaurant, pizza, and sandwich shops, even a sushi place. "But if you want to experience a week in Phantom's shoes, we'd better go to Denny's." She said this as if it were a mandatory assignment while she would prefer anything else on the list she'd rattled off. Then she smiled and, as if to talk both of us into it, added, "We can celebrate your visit with some milkshakes."

"I'm in," I smiled.

Without checking in with the hostess, we took a seat at the last booth in a narrow line of a dozen that led away from the front lobby. "This was his spot," Rennie told me.

I could see why. It offered a view of the kitchen, busy with aproned cooks churning out hamburgers and pancakes and hollering, "Table 25," over the chorus of clanging pots and pans. I pictured Phantom sinking into the same booth and filling the heavy air with stories.

Between taking orders and delivering plates stacked with greasy diner fare, the servers who knew Phantom best stopped by our table to greet Rennie and fulfill a request she'd made earlier in the week: that they talk with me for a few minutes about one of their most loyal customers.

"You know, there are others he knew better. But we'd talk some. Or, really, he'd talk, and I'd listen," José, one of the managers, offered as he set our milkshakes on the table. "He'd come in after fishing all day, and he'd tell me how he caught fifty trout in four hours and had to throw all but five back. Used to say he could predict the weather months, or even years, in advance." He tried to suppress a smile but failed, "I don't know about all that, but he always treated everyone here real nice."

He glanced over his shoulder at the busy dining room and said, "I'll take over for Erica so she can come talk to you." He waved over a woman who looked about my age. She approached with a curious smile. "Is this about Sierra Phantom?" she asked.

I introduced myself and told her I remembered him talking about delivering fish to "his girls at Denny's."

"He talked about me?" she interjected, her eyebrows raised.

"Yeah. Always said things like, 'I've got a few girls who are trying to fatten me up.'"

She smiled, and her eyes sparkled with humor. "That's for sure. Didn't work, though."

I took a sip of strawberry shake and asked her to tell me more about his fish deliveries.

"Well," she started. "It was probably three years ago now he asked me, 'You like fish?' I told him that my husband and I both love fish. So the next time he came in, he brought a big bag of trout. We had fish for weeks—we grilled it, broiled it, turned it into fish tacos and fish soup, anything we could think of. And I'd report back to him what we made that week with his catch and who we were sharing it with. He'd just light up, 'Well, I better get back out there to get ya more,' he'd say.

"From then on, he brought me a bag of fish once a week. When we couldn't fit any more in our freezer, we gave them to cousins, my sisters, our pastor, then my husband's aunt. It got to be so much that I ran out of places to store it while I was looking for someone who needed it. One day

I forgot about it and left it in the freezer here, and I got in trouble; one of our managers didn't want me keeping it here."

"Oh, that's not good," I added.

"Yeah, so now what I do—or what I was doing when he was still bringing me fish—I'd put ice in a big bucket by the back door, so I wouldn't forget to grab it on my way home. Then I'd figure out who wasn't sick of eating fish that week."

I followed her lead, and we both laughed.

"It was so sweet, but really it was way too much food," she smiled. "He was just sweet. He never flirted like some guys here do with us, he was just respectful, you know?"

I nodded.

"One night, my manager—not José, another one—said I could give him his meal for free. He wouldn't eat much anyway. So ever since then, I'd only charge him for part of his meal, maybe just the coffee or just the fries. I knew he lived on social security, so I'm sure he didn't have too much."

"Really?" I laughed. "Did your manager ever find out?"

"Well," she gave a quick look over her shoulder, "I just figured if she asked, I'd say, 'You never told me to stop giving him free meals.'" She tried to hold back a laugh. "And no matter what his meal came out to be, he'd leave me a dollar tip. By some standards, that's not much, you know."

I nodded and smiled, picturing how great a meal with Phantom would be.

"But I didn't mind," she said, and she paused as her eye caught another hurried server's. "Really, he gave a lot more to all of us."

After Erica and the others returned to their work minutes later, I started thinking over what José had said about Phantom's fishing tales and that he'd adopted psychic abilities when it came to the forecast. I hadn't heard that one yet. This wasn't the first time Journalism Rule #6 had come to mind: fact check everything. There's an old-time reporters' joke that says if your mother tells you she loves you, verify it.

"Rennie," I started before I could convince myself not to bring it up. "I was asking Ron at Mac's about some of Phantom's stories about living in the wild all those years."

"Mmhmm?"

"He says it all checks out."

"Oh yes, it does. He knew more about the High Sierra than anyone. You can't learn that stuff from guide books."

I nodded and stayed quiet a moment, as José delivered an iced tea for Rennie. Then added, "But what about the other stuff?"

Her lips formed a narrow, polite smile. Her fingers fished for a sugar packet among the collection of condiments. She slowly tore the top of the pink packet and dumped its fleeting contents into her tea. Still smiling, she finally said, "I've never known a person like Sierra Phantom."

She paused to take a sip of her tea. "But ya know," she laughed, "I doubt another man like that ever walked this earth." I thought she was avoiding my question and would move the conversation to the way he added a bit of glitter to practically everything he owned, to how he stockpiled canned vegetables, or to how he couldn't help but hold a soft spot for the underdogs of the world.

But instead she said, "You know, everything was right on the surface for him. He'd be so happy—about fishing or his garden or his guided tours—and in a snap he could be angry. And other times he'd call me in the middle of the night crying about who-knows-what, maybe old memories he couldn't shake. Then, suddenly he'd be over it." She paused a minute and took another sip of tea; then she looked up at me. "There's nothing phony about that."

I smiled gently and left it there.

CHAPTER

-30-

(n.) A symbol used by journalists to indicate the end of a story.

ONE OF MY REGULAR ASSIGNMENTS at my first job out of college was writing obituaries. It was always a task given to the newest reporter on staff as an exercise in learning the importance of details, like correctly spelling and punctuating a long list of surviving relatives.

My dad had died just a few months earlier, so to keep a safe emotional distance from the realities of the task at hand, I did my best to think of it as a formula. Each obituary had all the same elements, and I just filled in the blanks. It got to a point where I could mindlessly plug in the details of a person's life, their surviving loved ones, and the time, date, and place of the service in minutes. I pictured the same gathering over and over, at this or that church or this or that cemetery, followed by ham sandwich and potato salad lunches. In my mind, they were all cookie-cutter ceremonial goodbyes.

In true Sierra Phantom fashion, his was different.

It was one of my last days in Bishop, and Phantom's closest friends decided to hold a memorial service in one of his favorite spots on earth, South Lake. The unspoken dress code was jeans and T-shirts. The lunch was hot dogs and potato chips washed down with cold beers. The sanctuary was an expansive mountainous canyon surrounding 170 acres of cool blue water, and an eight-person pontoon served as the pew.

As Phantom's closest friends took turns climbing into the boat on a Friday afternoon, I introduced myself to each of them. Jared, a guy about my age who owned the only establishment on the lake, Parchers Resort, took the driver's seat. Then Ed and his wife, Patty, took their seats next to Rennie and her son, Mark. Finally, Brett, who worked at Parchers and fished with Phantom on his days off, sat down. I thanked them for inviting me to tag along on such an important day. They asked a bit about where I was from and how the week was going, and then together we moved the conversation to their friend.

Without being told, everyone had brought something to share in remembrance of him. Ed brought his fishing buddy's favorite belt buckle, and, of course, Phantom had painted "SIERRA" on it with green glitter glue.

"He wore this pretty much every day," Ed said, holding it up for us to see.

Rennie brought his ashes. She had the funeral home pack them in a nice wooden box, and she dressed the box in one of Phantom's favorite plaid shirts with snap buttons, which read "MOUNTAINEER" over one of the pockets and "SIERRA PHANTOM" over the other. Atop the box she set his cowboy hat decorated with fishing flies and glittered paint that was as colorful as he was.

Patty brought a stack of photographs and a folder full of newspaper clippings from the various times his name appeared in the Inyo Register. I flipped through them to find brief articles about his accidents, a picture of his neighbors and him in front of their garden, an article on his squash that won a blue ribbon at the Inyo County Fair, and a longform feature story on "a genuine mountaineer who's offering guided tours of the High Sierra." Patty had included four or five copies of his obituary and even a couple of small classified ads that he ran over the years, one asking for a ride down to UCLA for eye surgery and another, printed several weeks later, thanking the community for helping him get down there, but I think that was likely a message for Rennie.

Jared and Brett each brought fishing stories. They went on about some of Phantom's biggest catches, and Jared pointed out his favorite fishing spot on the other side of the lake, where he was slowly guiding the boat.

"He'd walk along the dam there and down those rocks to get to his spot," Jared said. "And, I'll tell ya, he was not happy if someone beat him to his spot, and he'd let them know." He laughed, and we laughed with him. "We saw him out there almost every day. Even last summer he was still doing that."

Brett said Phantom would take Parchers' boats out on occasion to see how the fish were biting on the side of the lake where the shores were too rocky to access by foot. "And oh man, a couple of summers ago, a huge thunderstorm rolled in while he was way out there. We thought everyone was in off the lake, but then we see this skinny dude driving a little boat in from the other side of the lake. We realized it was Phantom—he looked like a drowned rat. He wasn't driving the boat very straight at that point. He got to shore, and he was sopping wet and shaking cold," he smiled at the memory. "We actually took him down to the hospital because we thought he might have hypothermia. That's the kind of dedication he showed to fishing. Always the first one out, last one in."

As we reached the opposite side of the lake, Jared shut off the boat's motor and threw a small anchor overboard. We let silence settle over the boat for a few seconds as we swayed in the same water Phantom had pulled out hundreds of fish.

"This is what he'd want," Brett said. "He'll have this fishing spot forever now."

"Hell yeah," Jared added softly.

"I know you truly felt love here," Patty offered. "We'll miss ya, Sierra Phantom."

Ed began to sprinkle the ashes over the side of the boat. The dust rested on top of the calm lake a moment and then swirled through the clean mountain water down to the rocky bottom. Rennie handed each of us a handful of bright orange feathers she'd found in Phantom's briefcase. We each threw them over the edge of the boat to rest on top of the ashes. "See you in a couple days, dude," Ed said. "I'll be up here trying to catch that big trout that got away."

"No fish got away from Phantom," Jared added with a smile. Ed smiled and nodded.

Rennie, who stayed quiet while everyone else spoke his or her piece, sat up straight like she might want to add something. She pressed her lips together and finally said softly, "Bye, Phantom."

Her eyes stayed on the feathers slowly dancing above the water. Brett started to pull up the anchor but stopped when Rennie spoke again. "I miss you all the time," she whispered, not talking to anyone present. "We had such fun together, and you brought such joy to me." Then she looked up and smiled at me. "And the greatest gift of all is the new friends I have." She looked back at the feathers, now gathered along the rocks where Phantom had spent some of his favorite moments. "So rest in peace."

THE NEXT DAY, before my flight home, Rennie suggested we make a few final stops. She drove me past Pleasant Valley Reservoir, Phantom's go-to fishing spot in the colder months; the Paiute Palace Casino, where he bought his "all-natural smokes;" Raymond's Deli, the other place he liked to sell flies; and, finally, Valley Apartments.

"Want to jump out here?" she asked. I nodded.

She slowed the pickup to a stop on the side of Clarke Street in the shade of a giant cottonwood tree. The signs Phantom had ripped down were back up, neon orange lettering on flimsy black paper, firmly instructing "NO PARKING," preserving a patch of asphalt that was the centerpiece of the U-shaped apartment complex. They were nailed to a wooded awning, a whitewashed structure that looked like it was put there decades earlier as an attempt to make the place feel more welcoming. It offered a bit of shade for a small patio area and, I noticed as I walked closer, a garden.

I looked back at Rennie, motioned toward the garden, and smiled. Everything was just as he'd described it. Vegetables and f lowers were neatly planted in two large raised beds shaped into a "V". Little signs cut out of cardboard and glued to popsicle sticks neatly labeled the tomatoes, string beans, squash, and peppers. The dirt, which was the color of coffee grounds, was freshly watered, and not a weed could be seen.

His neighbors had kept up the garden. What Phantom called "a community garden." He must be beaming.

When I got back to the car, I told Rennie what it meant to be able to walk through a scene from his daily life. She smiled but stayed quiet, until finally saying, "You hungry?"

I laughed a little, "Sure." "You like Mexican food?"

"Yes, love it," I said with wide eyes. Virginia has a lot to offer in the way of seafood, fried chicken, and peanut soup, but good Mexican food, that seems to be the unofficial state cuisine of California, is hard to come by.

"Well, this won't tell ya much about Phantom because he didn't like Mexican food, but there's a little place down on Pine Street that's great. My treat."

Now, Journalism Rule # 7 is don't accept gifts. This is another rule of journalism ethics. You don't want to owe a source anything, even a lunch's worth of favorable reporting. My first editor, Eric, used to make me take everything from homemade cookies to flowers that sources would drop off as "thank you" gifts to either the homeless shelter or the hospital. I closely follow this rule to this day, no matter how tempting the gift may be. Even at those yawn-inducing legislative breakfasts and board retreats where it seems the only bit of fun are the donuts, I take nothing more than coffee.

But none of this crossed my mind as Rennie and I sipped margaritas and talked about the week's highlights. I was not on assignment. I was out to lunch with a friend. And I knew now what clinging to the rigid rules of journalism would have cost me. A bizarre mountaineer never would have entrusted me with his story. It's as if he dared me to abandon everything safe and predictable right along with him.

"You can treat this time," I told Rennie when the tab arrived, "as long as I can get us Schat's pastries before we take off."

"Sounds like a deal," she smiled.

"Thanks, Rennie." I raised my glass to offer a toast, "Here's to Sierra Phantom."

She paused a second to smile before adding, "To Phantom."

We sipped the last of our drinks and headed back to the trailer park so I could say bye to Mark and a few of the neighbors I'd become friends with during the week.

"Come back soon, all right," Mark said, giving me a brotherly bear hug. "And bring that husband of yours next time."

"I don't think that will take much convincing," I said as I hoisted my duffle bag over my shoulder and headed toward the truck. "One picture of South Lake and he'll book the next flight."

"Oh wait, I want to give you something," Rennie hollered from the driver's seat. "Mark, will you go in and grab those few things we talked about."

He smiled and hurried into the trailer. A few seconds later, he returned with his arms full of a few of Phantom's favorite earthly possessions: his cowboy hat, a pair of leather gloves and his jacket. He had etched each of them with glittered messages about the High Sierra and paintings of trout and eagles. Inside the jacket's pocket was a plastic sandwich bag full of glitter flies.

"Rennie," I looked her direction. "Are you sure?" "He'd want you to have it," she insisted with a grin.

I ran my finger along the glittered paint on his jacket and, unintentionally, took in a whiff of cigarette smoke. For half a second, I felt like I was in his presence.

I managed to muster, "wow, thank you."

"Hop in," Rennie chirped. "I thought of one more place you have to see. The bookstore."

"OK, sure."

Mark carefully set the treasure on top of my duffle bag while I climbed in. "It's not really a Phantom thing, but it's just cute," she continued. "You can grab us a couple of coffees to go with our pastries." "Sounds good." First she pulled into Schat's so I could fill a bag with croissants, cookies, and a loaf of sheepherder bread—I wanted to taste what the fuss was all about. Then she pulled back onto Main and directed us toward an alley near Phantom's apartment complex. I saw a small sign, "Spellbinder Books This Way," pointing to an inconspicuous rear entrance. She navigated the truck into a handicap parking spot and said, "You go ahead."

"OK, I'll make it quick."

The shop didn't seem to fit in with the Bishop scene. I don't know how else to describe it besides saying it was anything but quirky. It was cute and clean and organized in easy-to-navigate rows, with sections dedicated to local authors, children's books, outdoor adventure, and other genres. I strolled through the place and found a few shelves stocked with books about Bishop and the Sierra Nevada Mountains. I stacked my arms with little souvenirs—a book on the history of Bishop, a sepia-toned map of the region, a bookmarker, a stack of postcards—and made my way to the register.

"Are you a fan of Bishop?" the middle-aged woman behind the counter asked with a grin.

"Yeah, I guess I am," I smiled, looking over all I had dumped on the counter.

"Is this your first time here?" she asked, ringing up my purchase. "Yes, but I'm sure it won't be my last. It's a great town. It's so different than any other place I've been."

"Yeah, Bishop has that effect on people," she smiled as if she were talking about a favorite uncle.

"Actually, I'm here because I'm writing about a man named Sierra Phantom. Did you know him?" She started to shake her head no. "He had a long beard, always wore a cowboy hat," I added, "and sold his glitter flies at Schat's."

"Oh, yeah," her eyes brightened. "I mean, I didn't really know him. He'd stop in on occasion, browse through some of the books. I haven't seen him in a while, though."

"Yeah, so . . ." I broke the news.

"Oh, really? Man, I wish I would've gotten to know him. Seemed like a cool guy." She tossed my purchases in a plastic bag and said, "Twenty-one dollars and fifty cents."

I dug out my cash. "Yeah," she continued. "Bishop draws a lot of people like that."

"Like Phantom? Really?" I said in disbelief.

"Well, not exactly like him," she smiled and slipped my cash in the register.

"But it's like a magnet for really unique people, people who've lived through some stuff." She seemed to be avoiding a four-letter word. "I don't know what it is . . . seems like everyone here has a backstory."

I nodded without smiling. Because I didn't know her story, a smile didn't seem fitting. I thanked her and grabbed my bag of Bishop memorabilia.

"I'm sure he had quite the story," she said as I started to turn to leave. "That much is true." I stood for a second and smiled as I realized the importance of the moment, my last conversation in Bishop. I didn't want to ruin it with words, so I gave a quiet wave.

I made my way to the little coffee shop tucked in the back corner of the bookstore and ordered two lattes. As I sat waiting for the order, half-consciously letting the woman's comments settle in amidst the noise of the barista grinding coffee and steaming milk, the most important aspect of Phantom's story came into view. Out the window, I saw Rennie patiently waiting for me in her blue pickup truck, which I could hear rumbling, pumping out air conditioning to ease the harshness of a July day in the high desert.

Yes, a lot of Sierra Phantom's life is a story of survival, I thought. Literally, about facing the edge of where life ends and death begins and pushing his hardest to fall on the right side of that line. I think these people in Bishop, his friends who became his family, saw him as that survivor. They gradually learned he'd faced a hellish growing up, the front lines of battle, and the harsh elements of the High Sierra only to come out on the other side as the victor. But I don't think they realized that this was the first time he was allowed to do more than merely survive. In this place, with them, he lived. He loved. He was free.

THE END OF A SWINGIN' SAFARI

About the Author

Danielle Nadler grew up in South Dakota, where a patient writing teacher fostered in her a love for relevant story telling. As soon as she had a journalism degree in hand, she moved west in search of warmer weather and more exciting headlines. Her reporting has garnered first-place press association awards in California, Nevada and Virginia. Shortly after publishing Without a Trace, she and her husband became foster parents, hoping to provide a safe haven for the young Sierra Phantoms of the world. They live in Northern Virginia, where Danielle serves as managing editor of Loudoun Now, a community newspaper. Follow her work, and find photos and audio of her favorite subject, Sierra Phantom, at DanielleNadler.com.

Acknowledgments

Thank you first and foremost to the friends of Sierra Phantom, specifically Rennie McKinney, Travis Young, Jared Smith, Lauren Carrigan, Craig Davidson, and so many others who selflessly shared their time, talents and stories with me. You became partners in this dedication project.

I am grateful to so many who helped guide me through my first book: Zoe Reyes, for first seeing the value of Sierra Phantom's story; Derek and Lindsey Rice, for nudging me to see it through; my sister, Joy Navratil, for our late-night editing sessions; my brother-in-law, Nathaniel Navratil, for contributing his talents to design the book; and several others who carefully edited my work and generously offered their expertise, including Kristen Akina, Janelle Zander, Lisa Hughes, Rebecca Layne, Suzan Page Houser, John and Jennifer Read, Jeff and Jenny Kellogg, Hugh Weber, and Jennifer Steichen.

Thank you to the team at Morgan James Publishing for seeing the potential in an old man's story as told by a first-time author. Your willingness to take a risk on this project has meant thousands more carry Sierra Phantom's story.

I'm indebted to my parents, Caren MacMurchy and the late Robert MacMurchy, for first igniting in me a love for well-told stories. And thank you to my patient husband, Aaron, who did everything from extra household chores to solo grocery runs while a mountaineer on the opposite coast held my attention.

Resources

This is a work of literary nonfiction. I have worked to recreate scenes and conversations as accurately as possible using information gleaned from newspaper archives, historical records and interviews with Bishop-area journalists, fishermen, hikers, and other local experts. Some names and identifying factors have been changed to protect individual's privacy.

Sources include:

Fishin' Trails: 25 Short Hikes for Eastern Sierra Wild Trout and Fishin' Trails 2: 25 More Hikes for Eastern Sierra Wild Trout by Jared Smith

Images of America: Bishop by Pam Vaughan, Brendan Vaughan, and the Laws Railroad Museum

Images of America: The Owens Valley by Jane Wehrey

Inyo County Register, specifically articles, photos, and classified ads published Oct. 19, 2008, March 6, 2010; Feb. 7, 2012; and others Sierra Phantom and friends clipped and mailed to me that were not dated

The Sierra Reader, specifically the Feb. 9-15, 2012, issue

Sierra Wave Media, specifically articles published Oct. 20, 2008; March 6, 2009; and Feb. 20, 2012

Morgan James
Speakers Group

www.TheMorganJamesSpeakersGroup.com

We connect Morgan James published authors with live and online events and audiences who will benefit from their expertise.

Morgan James makes all of our titles available through the Library for All Charity Organization.

www.LibraryForAll.org

Printed in the USA
CPSIA information can be obtained
at www.ICGtesting.com
JSHW022218140824
68134JS00018B/1124